## ABOUT THE AUTHOR

Robin Bruce Lockhart is a Catholic convert and has built up his close relationship with the Carthusians over twenty-five years. He is the son of the late Sir Robert Bruce Lockhart, the author and former Deputy Under Secretary of State for Foreign Affairs. Throughout World War II the author served in the Royal Navy. Formerly a newspaper executive, first as foreign manager of the *Financial Times* and later of Beaverbrook newspapers, he now works in London as a stockbroker.

Robin Bruce Lockhart is the author of *Reilly — Ace of Spies*, recently the subject of a major TV series, and lives in Hove, Sussex, just fifteen miles from St. Hugh's Parkminster, the only Charterhouse in England.

# HALFWAY TO HEAVEN

ROBIN BRUCE LOCKHART

# HALFWAY TO HEAVEN

## The Hidden Life
## *of the Sublime Carthusians*

With a Foreword by Archbishop Bruno Heim

THE VANGUARD PRESS
New York

Copyright © 1985 by Robin Bruce Lockhart
Foreword copyright © 1985 by Archbishop Heim
Published by Vanguard Press, Inc.
424 Madison Avenue, New York, NY. 10017
First published in Great Britain by Methuen London Ltd

*Library of Congress Cataloging-in-Publication Data*
Lockhart, Robin Bruce.
    Halfway to heaven.

    Bibliography: p.
    Includes index.
    1. Carthusians — Spiritual life. I. Title.
BX3303.L63 1986        255'.71        86-1712
ISBN 0-8149-0922-1

Manufactured in the United States of America

This book is dedicated to all Carthusians,
past, present, and future, and also to the memory
of the late Dom Michael Hanbury, OSB,
who gave me the initial courage
to pick up my pen and write it.

# CONTENTS

## Contents

# LIST OF ILLUSTRATIONS

1. The Great Cloister. A Carthusian returning from church to his cell.
2. Communion at La Grande Chartreuse.
3. Pope John Paul II and the local diocesan Bishop of Cantanzaro with the Carthusians at La Torre in October 1984, on the eve of St Bruno's Feast Day, when the Pope prayed at St Bruno's tomb.
4. The chapel, two miles up the mountain from La Grande Chartreuse, which marks the site of St . Bruno's original foundation in 1084.
5. a. The church of the Charterhouse of the Transfiguration, Vermont, USA.
   b. An aerial view of St Hugh's Charterhouse, Sussex, England.
6. a. The Charterhouse of Notre-Dame de Portes, established in 1115.
   b. Carthusians in their stalls for Divine Office.
7. a. A Carthusian nun in the sixteenth-century great cloister in the Spanish Charterhouse at Benifaça.
   b. A Benifaça nun receives the ancient sacrament of Virginal Consecration, unique to the Carthusians.
8. a. A Carthusian at prayer in his cell in the Swiss Charterhouse at Valsainte.
   b. At manual work in a cell.

Acknowledgements and thanks for permission to reproduce photographs are due to the Carthusian Order for plates 2, 5a, 6b, 7a, 7b and 8a; to the author for plates 4 and 8b; to A. R. Grierson for plate 1; and to L'Osservatore Romano citta 'del Vaticano for plate 3.

# FOREWORD

It is strange that there is comparatively little written on an Order as old as that founded by St Bruno just nine hundred years ago.

On the other hand, however, the Carthusians do not invite attention, although in many their way of life might arouse curiosity. The way of life has changed little over those nine hundred years: the striving for perfect renunciation remains at the core of it, and so their silence and their mortification has become almost proverbial.

The Second Vatican Council's Pastoral Constitution on The Church in the Modern World ('Gaudium et Spes') examines the complex question of the relationship between Church and world and says that 'the Church, at once a visible assembly and a spiritual community, goes forward together with humanity and experiences the same earthly lot which the world does,' (N.40). Especially since the Lateran Treaty of 1929, when the Vatican was recognised as an autonomous member of the international community, the Church has played an important part in world affairs, and more than ever during the pontificate of Pope John Paul II the Church has become familiar to people in a new way, for many of the people who know of 'the Vatican' now do not have any faith. Nevertheless the Church makes itself heard and known among all peoples; it walks more freely and confidently alongside them.

One is tempted, perhaps, as a result, to regard the contemplative life as an anachronism. Surely it cannot be part of the real mission of the Church to the world? Should not these people be out preaching, be visible signs of the Kingdom of Heaven among us?

In his address to the Minister General of the Carthusians in May of this year, Pope John Paul II referred to the frenetic pace of life today: there is a great urgency about all things so that more and more can be crammed into life. But to what purpose? This is not enriching of life, merely filling it. And with so many demands and distractions, it is all the more difficult to find time for God, to look for the stillness where God is found.

They are to be envied, then, those who have found that calm by removing all other distractions. And this closeness to God is an important aspect of the life of the Church, for that is what we are all looking for in some way, to draw closer to the source of all life and holiness: this is where the universal search for happiness must end.

I welcome this book as a reminder to all of us who are so 'active' that more important than what we do is what we are, and that there are those who are blessed enough to have chosen a way of life that is simply being in the presence of God.

Archbishop Bruno B. Heim
Apostolic Pro-Nuncio

18 October, 1984

# INTRODUCTION

Attached to Madrid's Plaza de Toros, the world's most famous bull ring, is a small and beautiful chapel. Next to the chapel is an operating theatre. Before every *corrida* a matador will spend some time in the chapel in silent prayer, heedless of the noisy crowds round the bull ring. He prays that he will not end the afternoon gored or dying on the operating table next door, like other toreros before him, but that God will be with him in *El Momento de Verdad* – the Moment of Truth – when matador and bull face each other alone in the ring for the kill.

There can be few people in the world who do not at some time or times in their lives experience a moment or moments of truth – a realisation, to put it at its most simple, that they are in the presence of something beyond and greater than themselves. Such moments of truth may come when facing up to great personal danger, or grieving over the death of a loved one; they may also arise when contemplating a great work of art, listening to a symphony, gazing at the stars – or on one's knees in church.

Temporarily, these moments of truth take us out of our earthbound existence and awaken us to the deeper meanings and issues of life. Temporarily, we are brought into touch with the divine reality of God. Sadly, these glimpses of ultimate truth tend to slither away all too quickly, forgotten in the return to earthly life and all its man-made trappings.

If we could only make an effort of will to hold on to these moments of truth, and ruminate on them or 'contemplate' them, such moments could become hours, the hours days and eventually, perhaps, the days years. To the average man or woman this may seem very difficult, but there have been and still are men and women who have turned their very existences into whole lives of truth.

Some years ago, when I was beset with considerable personal anxieties, a friend suggested that a religious 'retreat' might be of help to me and an introduction to the Carthusian community at Parkminster in Sussex followed. As a strictly enclosed order, the Carthusians do not normally accept visitors for retreats, other than those aspiring to join the order, but providence was on my side: I spent a week in Parkminster.

Brought up as an Anglican, I was at the time largely ignorant of the ways of the Catholic Church and I knew absolutely nothing about the Carthusians except that they were monks of some kind. In the course of that first week in St Hugh's Charterhouse, just as the matador and the bull face each other alone in the bull ring, so did I meet God face to face. It was not only a personal moment of truth, but a realisation that the monks within the Charterhouse were living in one long, eternal moment of truth.

Providence had also given me as spiritual mentor during my first visit to Parkminster the late Dom Andrew Gray, of whom a leader of the Catholic Church once said to me: 'If there is such a person in the world today as a living saint, that man is Father Andrew.' In the words of Father Andrew my experience was: 'A *face à Dieu*. It is not necessarily a comforting experience at the time, as you have found out, but it is in the direction of peace. Truth is frightening, as we are so used to makeshifts of our own – and others' – contriving. Yet the truth is ultimate peace, deep down, which is rarely disturbed, although we may get all het up on top.' Despite many back-slidings and periodic neglect of faith on my part, that perception of total truth has never quite left me. And I never cease to marvel at the everlasting moment of truth that every Charterhouse is in itself.

On leaving Parkminster that first time, the whole world outside seemed utterly mad. Roads, cars, houses, telegraph poles ... all were futile when set alongside the knowledge that I now possessed, that within the Charterhouse walls lay eternal truth, eternal wisdom, eternal peace and eternal sanity. As Father Andrew had said to me: 'Peace is the gift of God; the world offers a poor alternative.' Only later did I come to learn that the Carthusian vocation was the highest to which man could be called.

It was several days before I had the courage to return to work. I thought of telling my general manager some white lie about being ill; instead, I told him the truth. Providence was still on my side: he was a Catholic and lent me Thomas Merton's famous book *Elected Silence*.[1] I found comfort in reading that Merton, after his first visit to the Cistercians, had also found the outside world totally 'lunatic'. I was further interested to note that, but for the absence of a Charterhouse in the United States at the time, Merton would have opted for a Carthusian as opposed to a Cistercian vocation.

I thought of the early Christians, the Desert Fathers, steeped in prayer and devoting their whole lives to the contemplation of God. I thought of how their 'descendants', the Carthusians, were living halfway to heaven – almost unnoticed by the rest of mankind – in a life of truth and happiness. I thought of the great need in this iconoclastic world of today for man to reach back two thousand years to the very seedbed of God made man, and recapture in its totality some of that truth which nourished the early

[1] Published in the United States and in other countries under the title *The Seven Storey Mountain: Elected Silence*, the title of the English edition, is believed to have been chosen, with Merton's agreement, by Evelyn Waugh.

Christians. I thought of how little people – even priests – knew of the great repository of truth which lay within the walls of a Charterhouse, and of the monks who seemed to represent signposts: 'This way to heaven, please' – witnesses to God's love. I thought of how much we could learn from them and of the benefit we could obtain by emulating them to a greater or lesser degree. In the words of Father Andrew: 'It is only the first step which is difficult because it is a little humbling, nothing more. But the view on the other side is worth it. God would like us all to be saints, yet how many of us shrink from that first humbling step.'

We are living in an era when, despite enormous social reforms, despite great activity in helping the poor and hungry, despite tremendous strides in medical care, despite improved education and despite all the efforts being made to achieve 'unity' among the Churches, our so-called civilisation abounds in violence, self-interest and self-indulgence. The hedonistic materialism of both the capitalist and socialist systems, with their constant erosion of moral truths and values, permeates our lives more and more. Comparing the pluses and the minuses, hundreds of thousands of priests and ministers of all denominations working actively throughout the centuries would appear to have achieved very little progress towards establishing a genuinely Christian way of life in the world. The attempts by some Churches and by some individual pastors to popularise religion by 'bringing it to the people' with folk masses and guitar-playing vicars may have had some success on the surface with the young, but most of these efforts would seem to be negated by the compromising approach to the non-Christian social trends of the present day.

How can the ordinary non-believing man in the street be convinced of Christianity when he sees Catholics, Anglicans, Baptists, Methodists, Presbyterians, Calvinists,

Quakers, Lutherans *et al* making different claims about the Christian faith? St Bruno, founder of the Carthusians, showed his monks how to live above such petty squabbling: on his deathbed, undaunted by the recent schism between Rome and Constantinople, he recited the creed in both Greek and Latin. And I remember well, a good many years ago, speaking to a Carthusian Father about some doubt I was entertaining at the time on the infallibility of the Pope. The comment I received, unexpected yet full of natural spiritual wisdom, was: 'You know, I really haven't got much time to think about such things – I am far too busy living in the lap of God. However, I'm sure that if the Pope ever did make a mistake, God would very quickly put it right.'

What is the fly in the ointment, because there certainly is one? Can it be that many of our active efforts from generation to generation, although not necessarily misdirected, have been built on shaky foundations? To mix another metaphor, can it be that we should go back to square one or, as the Americans say, return to first base?

For nearly nine hundred years now the Carthusians, descendants of the early Christians and the Desert Fathers, have been living firmly on square one, their souls cradled in the hand of God, unceasingly contemplating, worshipping and praying to divine reality. When we pray: '*Thy* Kingdom come', logically this must mean: '*Our* Kingdom go.' To the Carthusian, '*Our* Kingdom' just won't wash.

Deserting this world, so much of which pays no more than lip service to Christ's teaching, the Carthusian lives with, in and for God in prayer, silence and solitude. A Charterhouse is a powerhouse of prayer – bringing God down from heaven towards earth, and lifting up the world towards heaven. At every moment of the day and night, somewhere in the world, there is a contemplative community praying for God's mercy and forgiveness of the sins of the rest of the world. If the day were to come when these prayers were to cease, surely it would herald Armageddon.

The awe-inspiring high walls of a Carthusian enclosure seem to set its members apart even from other contemplatives. Because the world has been consistently shut out, the breath of God seems to emanate not only from the monks within but from every cell, every flagstone and every blade of grass encircled by the cloisters. Those who have been able to visit a Charterhouse will know how, immediately one steps inside the monastery walls, an awareness of God's presence and an immense peace seem to pervade one's whole being. Truth may be found in patches from time to time in the outside world, but the glimpses are quickly lost amid the pressures of life. Within the stillness of a Charterhouse such insights and the peace they engender remain permanent.

Because they live more in the next world than in this, the Carthusians have no wish to sing their own praises nor, in their humility and recognition that they are sinners along with all mankind, do they seek such praise. The ordinary man and woman know little or nothing about these beacons of prayer and, indeed, so self-effacing are those who live in Charterhouses that even the great mass of Catholic priests have only the sketchiest knowledge of the Carthusian way. It is my hope that, in lifting the veil which has for so long sheltered Carthusian reclusion, this book will be of inspirational benefit to all.

Of the Carthusians, Thomas Merton, who was no mean man of prayer himself, wrote: 'They are the ones who have gone the furthest, climbed the highest, lifted themselves up above all others, out of this world and concealed in God. All day long, except for offices in choir, the Carthusian is with God alone.' More recently, Cardinal Hume wrote:

While contemplatives make up only six per cent of all Holy Orders, this is the six per cent return on capital which God reserves for himself. Their life is a contract with God which brings down love into the world. To them prayer is as easy as breathing for the rest of us. They say: 'We pray for the rest of the world and we are quite certain we are helping. Proof is unnecessary; we know!'

The roots of Christian life were planted firmly by Christ in a bed of prayer and personal communion with God. If those roots are not continually watered with prayer, however much we may tend the foliage above ground which represents our active life, the tree will never flourish as God would wish it. Prayer and still more prayer together with far greater efforts to achieve intimate personal relationships with God, must be our first priority.

We cannot all be Carthusian monks or nuns, but we do have a very great deal to learn from them about how to pray. Perhaps, too, priests and those considering a religious vocation should ask themselves whether the Carthusian way might not be their way. Who knows the benefit that might accrue to the world if that 'six per cent return on capital which God reserved for himself' were to be measurably increased!

Many people have helped make this book possible. It was encouragement from some of the Benedictine monks of Prinknash Abbey – especially the late Dom Michael Hanbury – who complained, albeit gently, of the paucity of information about the Carthusians since the sixteenth century, which finally helped me overcome my trepidation about treading where angels do *not* fear to tread and to write this book at all. For hospitality and guidance while writing the first draft of the book, I must express my gratitude to Abbot Sillem and the monks of Quarr Abbey – in particular Father Charles Fitzsimons, in charge of the Quarr library. To all these people, and to Father John Tracy, SJ, and other members of the Jesuit community at

Farm Street, London, my thanks for their helpful comments and advice.

Above all I must express my joyful and heartfelt thanks to the Priors and monks, Prioresses and nuns, of the various Charterhouses I have visited and stayed at both in Europe and in America – in particular, the Prior and monks of St Hugh's Charterhouse, Parkminster. The unlimited assistance, courteous hospitality and unfailing patience I have received from members of the Carthusian Order over a period of many months, together with unprecedented access to books and documentation not normally available to the public, have been wonderful gifts which I shall treasure to the end of my days. This book is the only way in which I can, however inadequately, offer my gratitude to all the Carthusians in the world.

Although this book may be the most comprehensive yet written about the life and times of the Carthusians, there are some inevitable imperfections. The full story is not so much buried in the massive hidden archives of the order, but written in the hearts of Carthusians past and present; in its totality it is God's own secret.

# PART ONE

# PATRES NOSTRI

Long ago our ancestors sowed the seed of our faith in the field of our Church, and it would be quite incongruous if their descendants reap the weeds of error instead of the harvest of truth.

*St Vincent of Lerins, 430*

To far too many of us today the conception of a God with whom we can have a personal relationship seems so very intangible that amid the hurly-burly of life, even when we do think of God, he is infinitely distant. God in the form of Jesus Christ may be more meaningful to some but he is still exceedingly remote. Many wonder what the phrase 'Son of God' really means, query the veracity of the Gospels and ask themselves whether Matthew, Mark, Luke and John were real people. When were they born, when did they die? Where are the contemporary biographies of them and their families? Other people get bogged down in theological debate on such questions as the Holy Trinity. Still more wonder why Christianity is divided into innumerable denominations, most of which indulge to some extent, despite the present ecumenical movement, in internecine strife, yet all claim in different degrees to be repositories of revealed truth.

For a proper understanding of the Carthusian way of life and total commitment to God, it is essential to return to the grass roots of Christianity – the early Christians and the supreme examples which in thought, word and deed they have set us all. The first Christians were men and women who had had personal contact with the disciples or the Apostles' own disciples; men and women who had no doubts at all about their faith. The Middle East, Asia Minor and Greece were set alight with the fervour of those first followers of Christ. In their thousands they obeyed Christ's command to follow him, 'forsaking all others', happy to die, if necessary, as martyrs in the certitude of their faith. They left their homes, in towns or villages, to live in the desert away from the corruption of a pagan world in order to devote their whole lives to God, praying in the wilderness as had Christ, John the Baptist, Moses, Abraham and others before them. Then was the land overflowing with saints!

We have strayed sadly far from those days, but it is our great good fortune that so many of the writings of the 'Fathers of the Church', as the founders and leaders of the early Christian Church are known, have been preserved together with many contemporary biographies of them. How different the world would be today were we all to regain just a modicum of that spirituality, fervour and joy which erupted in and from the Fathers.

Let the puzzled or doubting soul meditate on this extract from the Introduction to Vol. I of *The Fathers of the Church:*

> The Apostolic Fathers wrote long before the great con-
> stitutional revolts of Constantinople and Canterbury from
> Rome had wrought their seemingly irreparable damage.
> In these primitive writings, as in a mirror, all Christians
> whose minds and will and souls are wholly set on the truth
> and way of life of Jesus Christ will find a dogmatic creed, a
> moral code, an ecclesiastical constitution and above all an
> inward character of devotional, supernatural, sacramental
> life, that is self-authenticating. In the presence of martyrs,
> saints, scholars and simple souls like Pope Clement of
> Rome, or Bishop Ignatius of Antioch, or Polycarp of
> Smyrna, or the author of the 'Didache', or the 'Shepherd'
> or the 'Letter of Diognetus', no one will feel inclined to

apply such labels as Romanism, or Byzantinism or Protestantism. . . . Men of towering genius, of heroic mould, all in many lands and in different ages. Men of diverse character, education, racial origin and political background, men inclined to defend their own brilliance and original opinions, and men who cherished customs of their own locality, sought and found a common life, a common bond of love, a common source of spiritual strength that would open frontiers and make them members of a single family.

Even those who take pride in the modern mind and contemporary mood will feel little sense of intellectual superiority when they meet the minds of men like Athanasius, Basil or Augustine. It will be still harder to entertain any feeling of moral superiority in the presence of men like Ignatius of Antioch, Cyprian of Carthage, or Chrysostom of Constantinople. The Apostolic Fathers included men who were both vigorous in debate and aggressive in tenacity to their convictions.

The early Christian writers were interpreters of the teachings of the Apostles in direct continuity from the Apostles, and they have shown us how firmly their lives were rooted in the teaching of both Old and New Testaments. Just as the Apostles give us the spirit of Christ, so do the Fathers give us the spirit of the Apostles.

Much of the lives and writings of these holy men was devoted to uncomplicated 'wordless' prayer, contemplating God in their hearts in silence and solitude. Here to convey something of the mystical spirituality of the Fathers are some examples of the best patristic writings. The first thoughts I highlight are extracted from the writings of St Ignatius of Antioch, who was taken to Rome to be thrown to the lions in about 110, some twelve years after the death of St John (the Apostle). He was a true mystic who lived near enough to the time of Christ to absorb the experience of the Christian mystery in its entirety. To the Christian community at Ephesus he wrote:

[5]

Better be silent and be, than speak without being ... he who so truly possesses the word of Jesus can hear even his very silence; then he will be perfect, acting by his word and making himself known by his silence. [And to the Christian community in Rome, he sent this message:] My earthly desire has been crucified, there is no more fire in me or love for material things, only the living water murmurs within me the words: 'Come to the Father'.

Other important early Christian literature includes the *Didache*, written about the year 80 and the earliest known document after the New Testament, the *Letter of Barnabas*,[1] the *Letter to the Philippians of the martyr St Polycarp*, and the teachings of an unknown writer called 'The Shepherd of Hermas', all written between about 80 and 120.

St Irenaeus (*c.* 140–202) thought deeply about the inseparability of the mystical and the concrete existence of the Church. He continually stressed to agnostics the harmony of the two Testaments. The unity of the divine plan was the centre of his meditations: 'All things are known in advance by the Father and then done by the Son in order, in harmony, and in the appropriate time.'

Another Father of the Church was St Clement of Alexandria, who died about 215. A highly cultured Greek, Clement wrote mainly for the unconverted. His lyrical prose, even in translation, has a magic quality: 'God has given the universe a musical arrangement. He has placed the dissonant elements under the discipline of harmony that the whole world may be a symphony in his ears.... He has orchestrated this pure concert of the universe.' In another beautiful passage, St Clement emphasises the need for 'wordless' prayer:

Grace and language have been given us to express and serve our thinking. But God hears the very soul and

---

[1] Not the Barnabas who was St Paul's companion.

spirit. . . . God does not demand of us words . . . he sees
the thoughts of us all at once. . . . We may then sometimes
raise to him our wordless prayer simply recollecting our
whole soul within itself.

The great prayer with which Clement ends his Epistle is
an echo of Christ's Eucharist and recalls the Jewish
Amidah[1] of the Eighteen Blessings. Indeed, much of what
the Fathers wrote is redolent of the background of Jewish
faith in their thinking. They remind us never to forget that
in Judaism lay the crèche of Christianity.

These writings, Jewish in texture and outlook, provide
a strong link – despite the inevitable differences – between
Christianity and Judaism. The Jewish contemplative
Philo of Alexandria, who lived at the same time as Christ,
paved the way for St Clement, Origen, St Gregory of
Nyssa and a long line of other Christian writers. And it is
clear that the mystical commentaries on the Old Testament by the Fathers relate closely to the Jewish Mid-
rashim.[2] All the great Jewish prophets insisted on the
transcendence of the infinite spirituality of Jehovah.

Many people, Christians and Jews alike, do not realise
that, right up to the sixth century, there were Judaistic–
Christian communities – that is to say Jewish religious
communities which accepted the Torah and Jewish law,
and Christ, at the same time.

Primitive Christianity included recruits from among
such circles as the Jewish community at Qumran.[3] The

[1] The main section of all Jewish obligatory prayers recited in a standing
position.
[2] Many Christians are probably unaware of how closely the Eucharist is
descended from the Jewish ritual known as a *berekah*, a benediction or 'last
blessing' of bread and the fruit of the vine, and which included the
ritualistic washing of hands. In the Last Supper Christ used the liturgy of
the synagogue, and the earliest formula of the mass was no more than a
collection of prayers of the Jewish rite with the occasional addition of
'through thy servant Jesus Christ' and the words of the consecration.
[3] It was at Qumran that the Dead Sea Scrolls were found.

early Christians had many features in common with the latter as regards spirituality, liturgy and ecclesiastical organisation. Accordingly, we must not be surprised to learn that those in Jerusalem who grouped around the Apostles had so many quasi-monastic characteristics.

A disciple of Clement and one of the greatest of early Christian writers was Origen, living in the middle of the third century. In his writings he leads us to mystical heights on a paradoxically calm journey with only a hint of the inner fire that consumed him. Origen's purpose was to detach the soul from the world, this life being but a shadow of true reality. More ascetic than Clement, he was much inspired by St John the Baptist's life in the desert. In common with most of the Fathers, Origen concentrated on the indissoluble link between the Old and New Testaments and he interpreted the prophesies of the Old Testament accordingly. It was Origen who gave a powerful stimulus to the expansion of monasticism in the Eastern, Greek, Church: 'So happy will they be', he wrote, 'who see God no longer through a glass, darkly, but face to face, pure of heart, bathed in the radiant light of wisdom.'

Another early saint who cried out for solitary prayer was St Cyprian, who died in about 258: 'Our Master has taught us to pray in secret and in out of the way places, in our own room. This is in accord with the spirit of faith which shows us that God is present everywhere.'

That great pillar of the Eastern Church, St Athanasius (295–373), like St Clement before him, was also concerned with the inability of words to express the mystery of man's relationship with God:

Man's speech is composed of syllables which have neither life nor efficacy. It does no more than signify the speaker's thoughts. It flows out and dies away; it has no reality whatever before it is spoken. Consequently, it neither lives nor works – it is not a man but only the speech of man

[8]

because man who is its father is himself by nature drawn out of nothing.

Mystical experience implies, *ipso facto*, true knowledge of wisdom, and St Gregory of Nazianzen (died *c*. 390) wrote of wisdom in these words:

Wherefore I have said to Wisdom, 'You are my sister,' I have worked at her and raised her to the limits of my strength. I long to crown myself with her as with a crown of grace and delight. I seek the gifts of Wisdom, that word which lives within us to lighten our intelligence and sweep the shadows from the path which leads to God.

Another St Gregory (of Nyssa – died *c*. 394), writing of spiritual advancement – the equivalent of an increase in wisdom – gives us these thoughts:

The soul goes on continually from one desire to another that is even greater. It advances continually towards the infinite on a journey that takes her higher at every step. Such a soul leaves all baser things behind as far as man is able, and penetrates the sanctuary of the knowledge of God.

One of the greatest of the Fathers was St Basil (*c*. 329–79), who laid down the principles for monastic communal ('cenobitic') life for the Eastern – today's Orthodox – Church. I quote only one passage from his writings, the sheer beauty of which comes from one whose life, born of contemplation, had brought him face to face with God:

Sometimes perhaps on a still night you will have gazed up at the inexpressible beauty of the stars and thought of the author of the universe. You will have wondered who it is sowed such flowers so prettily in the sky while here below necessity must take precedence over charm. Perhaps during the day too you have given thought to the endless array of wonders that take place under the sun, and have risen from visible beings to divine the invisible. If you

[9]

have done these things you are ready to hear what I have to say.... You will have knowledge of yourself, earthly by nature yet work of the hands of God. Together we shall be taught and instructed, we shall discover ourselves, we shall know God. We shall worship our Creator. We shall serve our Master. We shall give glory to the Father.

From the well-known works of St Augustine, of the fifth century, I also offer a single brief, yet penetrating, commentary on Psalm 41:

In the House of God, feasting is without end. Choirs of angels give an eternal concert in the face of God and the eternal presence communicates a joy that is never diminished.... Something of that everlasting and perpetual rejoicing reaches the ears of our heart. Something that is a marvel of harmony and sweetness, provided the voices of the world are hushed.

Only by analogy can St Augustine attempt to communicate his grasp of God's eternal presence. But the fact that he and all the Fathers had this grasp is made beautifully clear from the knowledge of the joys of contemplating divine reality which has come down to us in their writings. It is this grasp of the total reality of God and ultimate trust shown by the Fathers of the Church which has been and is mirrored in the lives of the Carthusians, past and present.

## II

# THE CALL OF THE DESERT

The wilderness and solitary places shall be
glad of them, and the desert shall rejoice and
blossom as a rose.

*Isaiah 35:1*

Among the members of the early Church was a large body
of men known as the Desert Fathers, sublime figures who
went to the desert as in a second Exodus; they were the
pioneers of Christian monasticism, which they established
as the mainspring of religious life. Some knowledge of
their way of life and their sanctity is a pre-requisite to
understanding their spiritual heirs of today – the Carthusian monks.

Though monasticism certainly existed before Christ,
the immediate progenitor of Christian monasticism was
John the Baptist. When he, Jesus and Paul went into the
desert, they were each being obedient to a deep instinct,
hallowed in the Old Testament, which goes back as far as
Elijah and beyond him even to Exodus. They were following the example set by the people of Qumran, who were
their contemporaries and the principal exponents of the
spirituality of the desert. The Dead Sea Scrolls make it
clear that there existed at Qumran a society of Jews separated from the mass of people, intent on leading a more
fervent life obeying the Law and in expectation of the
Kingdom of God. These survivors of Essenism, escaping
massacre by the Roman legions, were able to pass on some
of their traditions to the first ascetics of Christian

monasticism. St John the Baptist, therefore, stands right in the centre of the hourglass, where the broad sands of pre-Christian monasticism narrow down to a single figure before opening up again into the great story of Christian monasticism pioneered by the Desert Fathers.

Throughout the ages, when man has wished to draw nearer to God he has sought the desert and penance. Penance involves separation – as does prayer – from what is created earthly and human. To the Desert Fathers seeking God in the wilderness, St John the Baptist, Elias and the Apostles served as models. Humble, silent men of great elementary common sense, they had a deep under-standing of human nature and eschewed theological con-troversy and verbiage. Yet they were embracing a life that led them to explore the untrodden paths of the invisible spirit. Their cells were the furnace of Babylon in which, in the midst of flames, they found themselves with God.

By the end of the second century AD, many solitaries had gathered together in 'monasteries' in Palestine, Syria and especially in Egypt where, over the next two cen-turies, there was a positive explosion in monastic life when thousands flocked to the desert to establish monasteries where they could live in communities, or to create anchorite hermitages, in their fervour to follow the 'hidden life' of Christ.

Jesus Christ spent only about three years of his time on earth preaching. The rest of his life is known as the 'hidden life' – 'hidden' in this context means 'obscure', and the outstanding feature of Christ's time in Nazareth is the insignificance of this village, of which the outspoken Nathaniel even asked: 'Can anything good come out of Nazareth?' Christ's 'hidden life' of self-effacement in ob-scurity among the uncultured and uneducated people of Nazareth, in constant contemplation of God the Father, was his essential period of preparation before revealing himself to the world. Excluding the Passion, these years

[12]

were just as redemptive as the three years he spent preaching: in this long period he showed mankind, by example, how to practise ordinary virtues in ordinary life. Except when Christ went into the Temple, at about the age of twelve or thirteen, and said: 'I must go about my father's business', we hear nothing further about his religious life until he emerges to preach, nearly twenty years later.

Many of the Desert Fathers were illiterate but they did know parts of the Bible and, like many people who cannot read, they had excellent memories. They learnt the Psalms by heart and sat in their cells pondering over a verse or two while weaving baskets. John Cassian, who spent ten years in the solitude of the desert, tells of monks spending many hours each day slowly whispering over and over again a single verse of a Psalm such as 'O Lord come to my assistance, O Lord make haste to help me.' To Cassian, the monks of the desert seemed to be almost 'composing' the Psalms instead of reciting from memory; it was as if the Psalms had become part of themselves.

Such was the ancient monastic way of prayer, the actual words formed with the lips being merely an accompaniment to the real prayer that was going on deep within the soul. This constant simple and repetitive act of prayer induced a calm, contemplative state – a state in which the Holy Spirit could take over. The words spoken were analogous to the gentle beat of the wings of a hovering bird. After a while, with practice, there was no need to say anything at all; prayer would go on in the heart, as it were, all the time – the 'wordless' prayer of which St Clement of Alexandria wrote.

If the Psalms were the corner-stone of the Desert Fathers' prayers, it was because the authors of the Psalms were held to have been inspired by the Holy Spirit. The Psalms constituted the hymnal of the second Temple of Jerusalem and then, as now, were one of the principal links between the Jewish and Christian faiths. They are perhaps the most significant and influential collection of religious prayers ever written. Summing up the whole theology of the Old Testament, they have been used for centuries as the mainspring of both Jewish and Christian liturgical prayer. St Teresa of Avila stressed that it was through the Psalms that the highest peaks of contemplation could be reached. How else had the Fathers of the Desert found their way into the regions of mystical prayer except through the Psalter? Thomas Merton has described the Psalms as 'the bread miraculously provided by Christ to feed those who follow him into the wilderness'.

Probably the best known of all the Desert Fathers is St Antony of Egypt (250–356). The son of well-to-do parents, at the age of twenty he heard a sermon preached one day on Matthew 19:21 ('Go sell all thou hast ... follow me and thou shalt have treasure in Heaven'), whereupon he renounced everything for the life of a solitary in the desert. His ascetism was an example to all, and he is one of the principal forebears of western monasticism. For the story of St Antony we are indebted to St Athanasius (328–73) whose *Life of St Antony* is a vivid testimony to the former's love of solitude and silence. When Antony did speak, to quote St Athanasius: 'His speech was seasoned with divine wisdom.' We are fortunate, too, that seven letters of St Antony have come down to us. Like so many of the Desert Fathers, St Antony laid stress on the importance of the 'wordless' contemplative prayer when he wrote: 'It is not a perfect prayer if one is conscious of oneself or understands one's prayer.' And again: 'The man who trains himself in the peace of contemplation in the desert has freedom from three kinds of struggle: of hearing, sight and speech. He has but one fight to undertake, that of the heart.'

Serapion, another Desert Father but less well known than St Antony, went one better than the saint in following the precept 'Go sell all thou hast. . . .' He sold his book of

[14]

the Gospels and gave the proceeds to the hungry, saying: 'I have sold the book which told me to sell all that I had and give to the poor!'

The solitude and silence of the desert engendered great spirituality in the Fathers of the Desert who, through their writings, have handed down to us a legacy rich in wisdom and simple truths. I quote from but a few of them.

> Behold, my beloved, [Ammonas, a disciple of St Antony, in *c.* 350, wrote,] I have shown you the power of silence, how thoroughly it heals and how fully pleasing it is to God ... know that it is by silence that the saints grow, that it was because of silence that the power of God dwelt in them and because of silence that the mysteries of God were known to them.

In *The Ladder of Paradise* St John Climacus (379–449) wrote, 'Prayer is in its essence the meeting and union of man with God.' And again: 'One hair is enough to blur your sight, one little care is enough to destroy your solitude for solitude is stripping away your thoughts.' St Mark the Ascetic, who died *c.* 400, said, 'In solitude, I find the country of revelation in the height of divine contemplation.' On the same subject, Abba Poemen (died 450) wrote, 'What is it that conquers every difficulty that comes your way ... silence', and Isaac of Nineveh (died *c.* 680) said, 'Solitude is an ocean with wonderful pearls hidden in its depths.' Finally, a longer extract from the writings of Isaac of Syria:

> Many are avidly seeking but they alone find who remain in continual silence, Every man who delights in a multitude of words, even though he says admirable things, is empty within. If you love truth be a lover of silence. Silence like the sunlight will illuminate you in God and deliver you from the phantoms of ignorance. Silence will unite you with God himself. More than all things love silence, it brings you a fruit that tongue cannot describe. In the beginning we have to force ourselves to be silent and then

there is born something which draws us to silence. May God give you an experience of this something which is born of silence. If only you will practise this, untold light will dawn on you as a consequence. After a while a certain sweetness is born in the heart of this exercise and the body is drawn almost by force to remain in silence.

Many other Desert Fathers could be quoted: St Jerome (340–420), for instance, who translated the whole of the Bible from Hebrew into Latin while living in a cave at Bethlehem, has given us detailed description of desert hermits in his *Life of St Paul, the Hermit*. There are also the fourth-century *Apophthegmata*, an anthology of sayings of the Egyptian hermits, and the writings of Theodoret and St James the Assyrian.

What is clear from a study of those men of sublime prayer is that, as time went on, more and more emphasis came to be laid on contemplation and mystical experience, and on the explicitly held doctrine of God dwelling in the soul. The theory of quiet (*hescychia*, which translated means 'sweet repose') was gradually elaborated. To the Desert Father prayer was essentially a matter of contemplative unity with God in silence and solitude. In the last resort, mystic silence, ceaseless prayer and the very trial of solitude itself was his lasting liturgy to God in the depths of his soul.

It would be quite wrong to think that these holy men had retired into the desert to avoid the persecution meted out to Christians at the time. Although forbidden to do so, some actually returned to the towns, deliberately seeking martyrdom, and when the persecutions ceased the Desert Fathers did not return to the towns. On the contrary, ordinary Christians who had been in hiding in the towns now flocked to the desert to share in the purity of the Desert Fathers' lives. The desert population exploded again and whole new towns were built.

The Desert Fathers' method of contemplative prayer is

much used today by Orthodox monks when they muse on what is known as the Jesus Prayer: 'O Jesus, son of the living God, be merciful unto me poor sinner', or 'Lord Jesus Christ, Son of God, have mercy upon me.' Over the centuries, countless Orthodox priests and monks have built their spiritual life on the Jesus Prayer, and through it have entered into the deepest mysteries of spiritual knowledge. The Orthodox way of reciting the Jesus Prayer is to combine the words rhythmically with breathing, in a manner not unlike that employed in yoga when reciting a mantra. The harmonising of prayer with breathing was recommended centuries ago by Gregory of Sinai (*c.* 540–604). Some hundreds of years later, St Ignatius of Loyola was to write:

> Every time I breathe in, I should pray mentally saying one word of the 'Our Father' (or whatever prayer is recited) so that only one word is uttered between each breath and the next. In the space between one breath and the next, I dwell particularly on the meaning of the word or the person addressed or on my own worthlessness or on the great difference between the magnificence of that person and my own worthlessness.

Later still, the 'breathing prayer' was strongly recommended by the eminent Swiss psychiatrist Roger Vittos (1863–1925).[1]

The earliest extant written references to the Jesus Prayer are in the writings of St John Climacus, St Diadochus of Photice, St Nilus of Ancyra and St Isaias the Hermit, all of the fifth century. However, the Orthodox Church apart, the Jesus Prayer is also much used by Carthusians and other Catholic contemplatives and I have heard of it being recommended not only by Anglican priests, but also by those who are not practising members of any Church.

[1] A prolific writer, particularly well known for his *L'Angoisse de l'homme moderne.*

[17]

In the words of the late Archbishop Alban Goodier, SJ, the Desert Fathers 'drew thousands to permanent discipleship in their desert retreats through the force of their single-minded search for God'. In their simple life of ascetism and mystical prayer they dwelt on essentials. They shunned controversial theological theories just as they did the values of the decadent society of their times.

The Egyptian desert still contains some communities of monks – mainly Coptic and Orthodox. Monks have been living in the monastery of St Catherine,[1] at the foothills of Mount Sinai, ever since it was built early in the sixth century.

How difficult it is to write about saints forsaking treasures on earth for treasures in heaven, when today's civilisation seems hell-bent on laying up treasures on earth. There is, to use modern jargon, a communications problem, but one which could be overcome if people not only aspired to the sanctity of the early saints and fathers but also drew on their wisdom. Their writings are startlingly beautiful and in their simplicity for the most part make very easy reading. Although so much of their life was spent in silence, what they did have to say was always to the point.

From the desert, the great concept of the joys of spiritual life in the wilderness now spread all over Europe. In the West, this was mainly due to the influence of one man, John Cassian. He deserves a chapter to himself.

---

[1] It was here, in 1844, that the earliest manuscript of the New Testament – the *Codex Sinaiticus* – was found.

# III

## THE RECLUSE IN EUROPE

He sitteth alone and keepeth silence.

*Lamentations 3:28*

Before considering the influence of Cassian, the spearhead of organised mystical monasticism in Europe, it is important to understand that not only did the fire of the desert monasteries ignite men's hearts in Europe, but so did accounts of the anchorites of Egypt who lived in caves or in glades of trees in the Nile Valley. Christian recluses probably made their first appearance in Western Europe in the fourth century.[1] There are records of a hermit called John who lived in Chinon in France around AD 400, of St Lupicin, a solitary of some hundred years later, of the anchorite St Amand in the Limoges area, and of St Junien, who died in 535, after living for some years in a cell made vacant after St Amand's death. At Chartres we hear of a woman recluse – Monegarde, who died in 530 – and there are records of the hermit called Désiré who was living in the Charolais in 570, and Caluppan of the Auvergne in the same century.

These recluses were not in any way considered eccentrics. On the contrary they were much respected, and St Gregory, Bishop of Tours (*c*. 538–94), spent much time visiting them. Furthermore, as hermitic life spread from France to the rest of Western Europe, the Church prepared special legislation for it which was enacted at the

[1] It is known that two hermit monks from the Nitrian desert accompanied St Athanasius to Rome in 339.

Council of Toledo in 646; its main provision was that a would-be hermit should first spent a probationary period in a monastery so that his suitability for such an existence might be assessed.

The seventh-century recluses produced a further saint in the shape of St Bavon de Gand, and in the following century Eginon, Bishop of Verona, resigned his office to adopt the life of an anchorite. In Germany we hear of two ninth-century female recluses, Judith and Salome of Bavaria, and of the love which Bruno, Archbishop of Cologne (935–65), bore for the hermits within his dominion.

In time 'rules' came to be written for anchorites and the text still exists of a spiritual guide for hermits called the *Regula Solitaria*. Written by a ninth-century priest called Grimlaicus, it incorporated many of the ideas of the earlier writers including the Desert Fathers, St Benedict and, in particular, Julian Pomarius (died *c.* 498), the author of *De Vita Contemplativa*.

After the foundation of the Carthusian and Cistercian Orders in the eleventh century people continued to be drawn to an anchorite existence but their numbers decreased. An early prior of La Grande Chartreuse prescribed a rule for recluses, as did the English Cistercian Aelred de Rievaulx in the twelfth century. The lives of English recluses in the next century were largely governed by the *Regula Anchoretarum*, known in Old English as the *Ancren Riwle*, much of which was copied from Guiges'[1] *Consuetudines Cartusiae* (Customs of the Charterhouse) of 1128. As late as 1320 a census taken in Rome revealed that there were 260 recluses in the city. In the time of Pope Leo X (1513–21) four recluses even lived in a chapel at St Peter's.

It may seem strange today that normal, balanced men

---

[1] Guiges was the fifth prior of La Grande Chartreuse.

and women, with the approval of bishops, should deliberately have sought the life of a recluse, but the hearts of those who did were ablaze with the inspiration handed down to them by the Desert Fathers. They tasted the joys of solitude known to the saints, and saints a number of them became. Nevertheless a weakness crept into the lives of anchorites who lived close to townspeople on whom they depended for food. Although sealed up in a cell, many a recluse had a window through which he could still communicate with the public, and to this extent he was not leading a life of true solitude. Recluses are still found occasionally in Europe, but they are mostly eccentrics and outside the sponsorship of any Church.

The reason for this brief incursion into the history of the European anchorite will become apparent in later chapters. There we shall look at the hidden life of the Carthusians, who for some nine hundred years have been the spiritual heirs of the Desert Fathers.

# IV

# JOHN CASSIAN, TOWER OF DAVID

Take a short verse of a Psalm and it shall be a
shield and a buckler to you.

*John Cassian, c. 360–433*, The Conferences

John Cassian was born about 360, and although his
nationality has never been agreed he was certainly born
within the Roman Empire, most probably in Provence.
He received a good education and, while still a young man,
forsook the world to enter a monastery at Bethlehem. Here
he spent several years familiarising himself with the ways
of the monasteries of Syria, but, aware that the most
devout monasteries and most spiritual anchorites were to
be found in Egypt, eventually journeyed to the Egyptian
desert in about 386.

By spending seven years in Egypt travelling around the
hermitages and monasteries, Cassian became steeped in all
the customs and traditions of the Desert Fathers. From
those most holy ancient anchorites, Chaeremon (subsequently canonised), Nesteros and Joseph, he learned
much of the wisdom of the desert. The 'Discourses' from
these hermits on Perfection, God's Protection, Spiritual
Knowledge, Divine Gifts, Friendship, the Keeping of
Promises and Chastity, have all been handed down to us
by Cassian.

After his seven years in the desert, Cassian paid a brief
visit to Bethlehem before returning to Egypt. This time he
went to Scete, north-west of Cairo and three days' journey

into the Libyan Desert in the southern part of the Nitrian valley and, at that time, full of monasteries. Some were inhabited by monks living a communal, or cenobitic, existence together, while in others were to be found monks who had adopted a solitary mode of life, living in separate cells from which they would only emerge on Saturdays or Sundays to worship together in a central church. St Palladius estimated that in the Nitrian valley in Cassian's time there were over five thousand monks feasting on the truth of the absolute. In addition to Cassian's own descriptions of monastic life in the Nitrian valley, St Jerome, who visited him, also gives details in his *Epistles* of the lives of the monks in that part of Egypt.

Cassian left Egypt for the second and last time in about 400, and we next hear of him in Constantinople where he was ordained deacon by St Chrysostom. From Constantinople he made his way to Rome, where he took orders as a priest before going to Gaul and settling in Marseilles.

In the forest outside Marseilles Cassian helped to establish two monasteries, one for men, built over the tomb of St Victor, and the other for women, called St Saviour's. The French monks had tremendous respect for Cassian's vast store of information on monastic life in the desert, and it was in Marseilles that he wrote his two great works, *The Institutes*, at the request of Bishop Castor of Apt, and *The Conferences of the Fathers*, at the suggestion of St Honoratus, later Bishop of Arles.

*The Institutes* contain instructions for and advice on the organisation of a monastery and passed on all Cassian's profound knowledge of monasticism of the desert. It gives detailed accounts of monks' dress, methods of prayer and times for divine office, and stresses the great importance paid to the Psalms. In Book Two of *The Institutes* we read 'of the canonical system of the nocturnal prayers and Psalms', and find that the order of the day, so to speak, as laid down by Cassian differs very little from that practised

[23]

today by the Carthusians and indeed by other monastic orders. 'The soldier of Christ', writes Cassian, 'should next learn the system of the canonical prayers and Psalms, which was long ago arranged by the Holy Fathers in the east.' He refers to the need to chant the Psalms at night and details the numbers of Psalms to be sung each night, 'fixed ever so long ago' and applied in the monasteries of Palestine. It is doubtful whether anyone has ever expressed the meaning or purpose of the Psalms so clearly as Cassian.

The background to the various liturgical offices of prime etc., were set down not only by Cassian, but also by St Cyprian, who wrote:

> For upon the disciples at the third hour [*Terce*] the Holy Spirit descended ... moreover at the sixth [*Sext*] hour, Peter going up to the housetop was instructed as well by the sign as by the word of God ... and from the sixth hour until the ninth [*Nones*], the Lord being crucified washed away our sins by his blood ... for we must also pray in the morning [*Prime*] also at the sunsetting [*Vespers*] and the decline of day [*Compline*] we must pray again.

Cassian also drew special attention to Psalm 119: 'At midnight [Matins/Lauds] I rose to give thanks unto thee', and 'seven times a day have I praised thee'.

In *The Institutes* Cassian wrote: 'Let your new monastery in its untrained infancy in Christ be instructed in the most ancient institutions of the earliest Fathers.... Fastings and vigils, meditation on scripture, poverty and the privation of all things are not perfection but the instruments for acquiring it.'

Cassian's *Conferences* expands the ethics of the Alexandrian traditions of the Christian platonists[1] – Clement and Origen – and from his frequent references to St Antony

---

[1] The early Christian writers found much in Platonism to help them understand Christian theology. The Alexandrian Christian scholars adapted Plato's philosophy to religious instruction.

it can be seen that this saint had imprinted much of his own spirituality on Cassian.

Cassian was a true mystic and, in attempting to describe mysticism, he wrote:

> It surpasses all human senses, the sound of voices, the movement of tongue, the articulate word. The soul wholly bathed in the light from on high no longer makes use of human speech, always so weak. It is a gazing on God alone – a great fire of love. The soul here is buried, engulfed in holy delectation and converses with him as with a father, most familiarly and tenderly.

He referred to a 'ladder of contemplation', consisting of three rungs. The first rung was contemplation of many things, the second rung was the contemplation of a few things, and the third rung was the contemplation of One alone in 'pure' or 'wordless' prayer. And it was Cassian who wrote – not with any intention of detracting from cenobitic life: 'The cenobite cannot attain to the fullness of contemplative purity.'

Cassian – or St John Cassian as he was to become – died in 433, and his body was buried in the church of St Victor in Marseilles. His influence on western monasticism through the centuries has been immense right down to the present day. Even a cursory study of St Benedict's Rule shows how much it owes to Cassian – it was St Benedict who recommended to monks the daily reading after supper of Cassian's *Conferences*.

Among the many spiritual thinkers and writers of later generations who acknowledge their great debt to Cassian are SS Benedict, Thomas Aquinas, Teresa of Avila, Ignatius of Loyola, ·Francis de Sales and Bruno, the founder of the Carthusian Order. A twentieth-century Carthusian has written of Cassian: 'It is impossible to overestimate the extent of his influence. Every generation of monks has been nourished by his works.'

# PART TWO

# V

# ST BRUNO, FOUNDER OF
# THE CARTHUSIANS

Of all the saints, St Bruno, founder of the
Carthusians, is the one above all who deserves
the epithet 'Great'.

*Alban Butler,* Lives of the Saints

Although a native of Cologne, Bruno Hartenfaust was a
Frenchman both by temperament and by upbringing.
Born in about 1030 of parents as pious as they were noble
of birth, he left Cologne at an early age for France where
he studied in Rheims, Paris and Tours. As a young man
his first interest lay in theology, and on completion of his
studies he took holy orders.

Bruno first gave himself to an active apostolic ministry,
and his zeal was such that he attracted attention throughout France. The Archbishop of Rheims was so impressed
by him that he took him into his personal service, confer-
ring on him the office of Chancellor – as master of the
cathedral schools. Bruno's twenty years in charge of these
schools gained him a high and far-reaching reputation,
and after his death it was written of him: 'Among masters
he was glorious and a living rule for life. . . . From his
schools there flowed forth over the whole world a great
stream of wisdom.'

Nevertheless he tired of the political aspects of religious
life which had developed in Rheims and, deciding that a
monastic vocation would be more meaningful, left for
Molesmes where St Robert and some friends had already

[29]

begun the monastic reform which was eventually to develop into the Cistercian Order. Here, under the guidance of Robert, Bruno passed his apprenticeship into monastic life. However, Bruno found that even Molesmes was but a halfway house. The Holy Spirit was driving him towards a deeper retirement and that hidden life of solitude in which he could bring to fruition the plans with which God was inspiring him. Leaving Molesmes, he went to a lonely spot in the forest of Sèche-Fontaine, but when followers began to gather round him there, including some from Molesmes itself, he decided to go still further afield in search of somewhere quite unknown.

It was in June 1084 that Bruno, guided by divine providence, took the road towards Grenoble with six companions: four in holy orders – Lanwin, Stephen of Bourges, Stephen of Die, and Hugh – and two laymen, Andrew and Guerin. At Grenoble Bruno sought help from St Hugh,[1] the bishop, in finding some deserted place where they could settle. Hugh is reported to have said to them: 'The site which Heaven seems to have marked out for you is a wilderness lost in the mountains. It is called La Chartreuse.[2] It is extensive enough, doubtless, but uninhabited – except by wild beasts. It resembles a prison more than a dwelling place and I do not believe that without special aid from Providence, anyone could live there.'

Bruno and his companions were undeterred by these remarks and it was Hugh himself who led them to the site. A chapel known today as Notre-Dame de Casalibus marks the spot; it lies in a narrow valley some four thousand feet above sea-level, shut in on all sides by mountains. Here

---

[1] Tradition has it that, prior to Bruno's arrival at Grenoble, Hugh had a dream in which he saw heavenly spirits erecting a temple on the site of La Grand Chartreuse. *The Dream of St Hugh* is the subject of a fine painting by Vincente Carduccio (1576–1638), now in the National Gallery of Scotland.

[2] Originally called Chatrousse and also Caruse.

Bruno's little band built some rough log cabins, on the lines of the ancient 'lauras'[1] of Palestine, encircling a small chapel. In this mountain desert their souls could soar aloft in freedom into the divine realms of contemplation which they sought. They realised to the letter the ideal life set forth by St Paul in his Second Epistle to the Corinthians: 'Let us show ourselves as the ministers of God in much patience, in labours, in watchings, in fastings, in chastity, in knowledge – sorrowful yet always rejoicing, having nothing yet possessing all things.'

Then, in the spring of 1090, a messenger arrived at La Chartreuse with a letter from Pope Urban II – a former pupil of Bruno's at Rheims – ordering him to Rome. The Pope had need of his counsel and help in the government of the Church. Although this testified to Bruno's learning and wisdom, the Pope's command distressed him and his fellow monks, whose numbers had increased during the six years Bruno had been at La Chartreuse. When he left for Rome some of his monks accompanied him, while others dispersed. The hermitage in the mountains was unoccupied for about a year, at the end of which those monks who had gone to Rome returned in sorrow without their guiding spirit. Lanwin was appointed prior in Bruno's place.

It was a difficult period for the Church, with schismatic elements in both Italy and Germany and with the Moslem threat to Christendom in the east. The Pope did little without first seeking Bruno's advice, and the fact that the situation in the Church was gradually stabilised was in part due to Bruno's wise counsel.

Bruno yearned to return to the solitude of La Chartreuse and refused the Pope's offer of the Archbishopric of

[1] Lauras were the names given to the groups of cells in which the monks of Palestine and Egypt lived. They are believed to have been first established there by St Chariton (died *c*. 350) at Pharon, north-east of Jerusalem, but may well date from earlier times.

Reggio. When Urban II eventually did allow Bruno to leave the papal court and resume a solitary life, to Bruno's sadness he stipulated that any new hermitage Bruno might establish should be in Italy. It was therefore in Italy, towards the end of 1091, that Bruno retired to set about founding the second Charterhouse at La Torre in Calabria.

Here Bruno built cells on the lines of those at La Chartreuse, but his efforts to resume life alone with God were periodically interrupted by the Pope who insisted on Bruno accompanying him to various ecclesiastical councils as adviser. Only after his return from such a council at Clermont in France did the Pope finally allow Bruno to enclose himself for life in the monastery at La Torre, never to see La Chartreuse again. His one-time companion Lanwin, now prior at La Chartreuse, journeyed to Italy to see him and together, at La Torre, they took counsel for the future interests of their small flocks in France and Italy, little realising that they were developing a great religious order – the unsinkable flagship of monasticism in the Catholic Church. Landwin made copious notes of his discussions with Bruno and these served as a basis for the *Consuetudines Cartusiae* which Guiges wrote some years later, and which have been the guidelines for Carthusian statutes down the years ever since.

Of Bruno's writings, sadly only two letters have come down to us – both written from Calabria in about 1099. One letter consisted of spiritual advice to the Brothers at La Grande Chartreuse, and the other was to his friend, Raoul le Verd, then at Rheims Cathedral and subsequently archbishop. The sheer sanctity of Bruno stands out in this extract from his letter to Raoul le Verd:

> I live in a desert quite a long way from any human habitation. What advantages and delights solitude and the silence of the hermitage bring to those who love it, they alone know who have had experience of it. It is there that generous souls can turn themselves inwardly as they will.

They can dwell apart and attend uninterruptedly to the cultivation of the seeds of virtue and happily eat of the fruit of Paradise . . . that peace I mean that the world knows not and with joy in the Holy Ghost. . . . O my brother, would that you loved only to be held in its embrace and burn with divine love.

To the Brothers at La Grande Chartreuse, Bruno wrote:

Of you, dearest brothers, I say, my soul proclaims the greatness of the Lord but I see the richness of his mercy towards you for we rejoice that the mighty God himself, since you are ignorant of letters, is writing directly on your hearts, not only Love but also knowledge of his Holy Law. Indeed what you love, what you know, is shown by what you do. It is clear that you are wisely harvesting the sacred scriptures' sweetest and most life-giving fruit since you observe with great care and zeal that true obedience which is the carrying out of God's commands – the key to the whole spiritual life and a guarantee of its authenticity. It is never found without deep humility and outstanding patience, and is always accompanied by pure love for God, and true charity. Continue therefore, my brothers, in the state which you have obtained.

Bruno's constant meditation on eternity animated him with a fervour and a spirit of penance which made him pass whole nights in tears, calling down God from heaven to extend his mercy to the whole world. His devoutness was of that same primitive freshness which had characterised the saints across the centuries.

Bruno died on Sunday 6 October in 1101. He was about seventy and it was seventeen years since he had left the world to found the Carthusian Order. When he felt his last hour approaching, like the patriarchs of old he gathered his fellow monks around him in the cave which served him as a cell. There they stood about the dying figure who was stretched out on bare boards covered with ashes. On the cave which was his tomb were inscribed the words: '*Haec sunt ossa magistri Brunonis'* ('These are the bones of Bruno, master of this hermitage').

Many miracles occurred at Bruno's tomb, but true to their principles the Carthusians made no effort to obtain his canonisation. The memory of him was kept as a priceless heirloom, and it was only in 1514 that the order asked Pope Leo X's permission to celebrate a feast day for him. Leo dispensed with any formal process of canonisation and immediately inscribed Bruno among the saints by a personal act of infallible authority. In the following century Pope Gregory XV made the cult of St Bruno obligatory throughout the Church. His feast day, which is celebrated throughout the Church, is 6 October.

VI

# FROM ST BRUNO TO THE
# REFORMATION

Monks and Oaks are immortal.

*J. B. H. Lacordiere, OP, 1802–61*

There is a Carthusian motto outlining the objective of
their vocation which runs: '*Non sanctos patefacere sed mul-
tos santos facere.*' The English translation is: 'To make
many saints but not to publicise them.' Before exploring
the meaningfulness of the Carthusian life to the monks
themselves and to the world at large, it is essential to
examine something of the history of the order – the back-
drop, so to speak, against which these holy men have lived
and died – and do live and die – in a kind of spiritual
stratosphere. They have rightly been eulogised by saints
and popes for their perfect spirituality, and as the only
religious order 'never to have been reformed because never
deformed'.[1] It was of the Carthusians that Pope John
XXII wrote:

> Great miracles of the world, men living in the flesh as out
> of the flesh. The angels of the world representing St John
> the Baptist living in the Wilderness. The greatest orna-
> ment of the Church. Eagles soaring up to heaven whose
> state is justly preferred to the institution of all other
> religious Orders, the heart of the Church. It is the most
> perfect model of a penitential and contemplative state.

[1] While it is true that the Carthusians are the only order never to have been
formally reformed, this is the result of their constant internal reformation
which suppresses at birth the slightest tendency to deviate from the
original Carthusian principles.

[35]

In the eleventh and twelfth centuries, nearly all the monastic communities followed the Rule of St Benedict in one form or another, but Bruno's prescription for his monks was distilled from many sources. While taking to him some of St Benedict's principles, he reached further back to the Apostolic and Desert Fathers themselves: St Antony, St Jerome, St Basil, St Pachomius and to Cassian and *The Rule of the Master* (author unknown). He blended all into one glorious recipe for the would-be saint. The imprint of Cassian looms large partly because of Bruno's own respect for him but probably also because two of Bruno's original six companions came from the now extinct order of St Ruf (secularised in 1773). This order had inherited much of the spirit not only of St Augustine but also of that of the monks of St Victor at Marseilles, a community which Cassian himself had founded.

Guiges, prior of La Grande Chartreuse from 1109 to 1136, set down in writing in 1128 all Bruno's precepts for what had now become an established order of monks.[1] As already made clear, his *Consuetudines Cartusiae* have formed the basis of all Carthusian Statutes ever since.[2]

In the *Consuetudines*, influences can also be found of the Rules of Grimlaicus, of the hermit monks founded by St Honoratus on the island of Lerins in about 400, and of the Rule of St Caesarius of Arles – a former monk of Lerins. Guiges points out that the *Consuetudines* relied additionally on 'other writings of incontestable authority'.

Summing up, the *Consuetudines* were distilled from the ideas of many saints to provide for the vocation of the call of the desert. In the words of a twentieth-century Carthusian: 'It is only the "Law" of the desert which has maintained the purity of our vocation with its permanent cell.' In so far as Carthusian life is at all communal, it is solely so as to facilitate a solitary life.

[1] The first General Chapter of the order was held in 1140.
[2] The latest Carthusian Statutes date from 1971.

It is a paradox that St Benedict, for whom Bruno and the early Carthusians had great respect, should have led a hermitic life himself yet write a rule for monks the basis of which was totally cenobitic, prescribing a life in which monks slept in communal dormitories. Despite this, it is clear that St Benedict considered the solitary life the highest of vocations, since he wrote:

> Men not in the first fervour of conversion, but after long probation in the monastery come well trained to leave the ranks of their brethren for single combat. Secure now without the consolation of a comrade they are able to live with God single-handed both night and day in sure knowledge of eternal life every hour of the day.

Within a century of Bruno's death thirty-three Charterhouses had been established, of which Guiges had been responsible for founding half a dozen, in line with Bruno's original plans which were for each community to consist of thirteen monks – symbolic of Christ and the Apostles – living in separate cells built round an oratory, together with a number of lay brothers. The total number in any community was not to exceed that which it could support without resort to seeking alms. If La Grande Chartreuse was the cradle of the Carthusian Order and La Torre its nursery, the Order quickly passed through adolescence into maturity when the *Consuetudines* received the formal approval of Pope Innocent II in 1133, thirty-two years after Bruno's death.

Peter the Venerable, the well-known Abbot of Cluny, describing the life of the Carthusians some forty years after Bruno's death, wrote:

> Their dress is meaner and poorer than that of other monks, so short, and so scanty and so rough that the very sight affrights one. They wear coarse hair shirts next to the skin. They fast almost perpetually, eat only bran bread, never touch flesh, either sick or well, never buy fish but eat it if given them as alms, eat eggs and cheese on Sundays

[37]

and Thursdays. On Tuesdays and Saturdays their fare is pulse or boiled herbs. On Mondays, Wednesdays and Fridays they take nothing but bread and water and they have only one meal per day except at Christmas, Easter and Whitsun, Epiphany and some other festivals. Their constant occupation is praying, reading and manual labour which consists chiefly of transcribing books. They say the lesser hours of the Divine Office in their cells at the time the bell rings but meet together at Vespers and Matins with wonderful recollection.

In the early days of the Carthusian Order, for the greater part of the year the ordained monks were normally only allowed to attend conventual Mass once a week, and the Brothers took communion no more than once a month. Although this may seem strange to us today, it conformed closely to the practices of the Desert Fathers. Whereas Mass was naturally always celebrated with due reverence, it was originally thought that too many Masses would interfere with a monk's personal and solitary contemplation of God. There will always be souls who tend to find a deeper peace and absorption in the presence of God when they are silent and alone, than when they are praying with others. However, after the Order had been in existence for about a hundred years daily Mass became the norm. Recently there has been some discussion within the Order on the possibility of reducing the number of Masses so as to conform more with original customs.

During the Middle Ages monks from Benedictine and other communities – but not the Carthusians – tended to mix with the world outside their walls and became rich. Regrettably, too, there was a good deal of corruption. Yet as the other monastic orders degenerated when the monks were permitted to wander the world in imitation of the new active orders, such as the Dominicans and the Franciscans, the strict and frugal Carthusians prospered, and the two hundred years between 1350 and 1550 was the period of the Order's greatest expansion. Concentrated originally in France, Charterhouses sprang up in the Low Countries, in Germany, in Spain, in Italy and in England. In a period of general religious decline during the Middle Ages, the more spiritual monarchs and well-to-do either founded or supported Charterhouses in their eagerness to establish reliable centres of prayer.

It was Henry II who founded the first English Charterhouse at Witham in Somerset in 1178, as penance for his part in the murder of Thomas à Becket; the Prior, who came over from La Grande Chartreuse, was later to become St Hugh of Lincoln.[1] Other Charterhouses established in England were those at Hinton in Somerset, Coventry, Kingston upon Hull, Axholme in Lincoln, Mountgrace at the foot of the Cleveland Hills in Yorkshire, Sheen in Surrey, and of course the most famous of all – the London Charterhouse.

At the time of the Reformation there were some two hundred Charterhouses in Europe, but then over forty houses were suppressed and fifty Carthusians, including the eighteen English martyrs, gave their lives for their faith. Carthusian blood flowed in England, France, the Low Countries, present-day Yugoslavia and Austria. Carthusians were also slaughtered by the Turks, and in 1562 La Grande Chartreuse itself was destroyed by the Huguenots.

Because their steadfast spirituality and incorruptibility gave them an influence out of all proportion to their relatively small numbers, the Carthusians became a prime target for destruction during the Reformation. And the almost unbelievable treatment meted out to the Carthusian martyrs in England is so shameful that few English

---

[1] St Hugh was the only Carthusian to become a bishop in England and the first Carthusian anywhere to be canonised. The application for his canonisation was made not by the Carthusians but by the English bishops.

[39]

historians will soil their pages with the story. But told it must be.

When Henry VIII confronted the Church with his determination to rid himself of Catherine of Aragon it was undoubtedly the Carthusians' faithfulness to discipline which enabled them to stand firm in the time of testing. At the time when John Houghton was prior of the London Charterhouse, in 1531, the King's application to the Pope for an annulment of his childless marriage to Catherine had reached a state of deadlock. Thomas Cromwell, who had succeeded Wolsey as Lord Chancellor, suggested to Henry that he should declare himself Supreme Head of the English Church and obtain a divorce from his own ecclesiastical court.

In 1533 matters came to a head. Anne Boleyn was pregnant and if the hoped for male heir was to be legitimate no time could be lost. Thomas Cranmer, who supported Henry's case, was made Archbishop of Canterbury and immediately pronounced his marriage to Catherine null and void. A few days later Henry married Anne Boleyn and she was crowned queen at Westminster Abbey. Public opinion rallied to the wronged wife, Catherine, and the birth of a girl, Elizabeth, to Anne Boleyn did not help; all this trouble and no male heir. Then came Rome's declaration that the marriage to Catherine was a valid one. The Act of Succession of 1534, asserting the nullity of Henry's marriage to Catherine and the validity of the new marriage, was an explicit defiance of the Pope and stipulated that every subject of the King, if called upon, should swear an oath of acceptance of the Act.

Within a month of the passing of the Act Thomas Cromwell's agents appeared at the London Charterhouse demanding that the community should take the oath. Prior Houghton, while realising the implications, refused to do so but tried to avoid disaster by claiming that it was none of the Carthusians' business. This did not satisfy

Cromwell, and Houghton, together with his procurator, Humphrey Middlemore, were taken immediately to the Tower. Here they were visited by the Archbishop of York, who half persuaded them that the oath did not involve matters of faith. They half accepted it by adding to the oath the words 'so far as the law of God allows', and were set free. This was not good enough for Henry and Cromwell. A further piece of legislation, the Act of Supremacy, was passed which made the King head of the Church in matters of doctrine as well as discipline; anyone not accepting this would be guilty of treason, punishable by death.

Prior Houghton assembled all his monks, and after three days of prayer, ending with a mass to the Holy Ghost, they prepared for death. Priors from two other Carthusian monasteries came to London and, together with Houghton, decided to ask Cromwell to leave their priories alone to serve God in peace and silence. By this time Cromwell, although a layman, had assumed the office of vicar-general of the Church, and nothing that the priors offered would satisfy him except complete acceptance of the Act. On their refusal they were taken to the Tower, where Cardinal Fisher and Sir Thomas More were already lodged as prisoners.

Ten days later the Carthusians stood trial in Westminster Hall. For two days the jury stubbornly refused to return a verdict until Cromwell threatened to indict the jurymen themselves of treason if they did not find the Carthusians guilty. This dreadful and shameful verdict was accordingly passed.

A few days later, on 4 May 1535, the three priors were taken from their dungeons, lashed down on wattle hurdles and drawn by horses over the dirty cobbles of the London streets from the Tower to Tyburn gallows at what is now Marble Arch. From a small window in the Tower, Sir Thomas More watched them go by; two months later his own head was to be on the block. Prior Houghton was the first to die; his last words were: 'Our Holy Mother the Church has decreed otherwise than the King and Parliament have decreed and, therefore, rather than disobey the Church we are ready to suffer.'

At Tyburn these holy men, who sought nothing but to serve God in silence and solitude, were half hung, disembowelled while still alive, dismembered and their heads boiled in oil. When the bloody butchery was over, part of Prior Houghton's body was nailed to the London Charterhouse gate in the hope that the gruesome sight would induce the rest of the community to yield.

But this was only the beginning. On the same day, one of Cromwell's agents made yet another unsuccessful effort to persuade the remaining grief-stricken Carthusians to deny their faith. Three more Carthusians were taken to Marshalsea prison and chained to pillars night and day. It is said that Henry VIII himself visited them in an attempt to get the monks to acknowledge his supremacy to the Church. They preferred a martyr's death and on 19 June, 1535, they were hung, drawn and quartered at Tyburn. The whole of Europe was aghast.

The King's hopes that, deprived of their 'captains', the remaining monks at the London Charterhouse would weaken were to remain unfulfilled. Efforts made by various emissaries of Henry over the next two years to undermine their faith were of no avail. Finally, in May, 1537, Cromwell gave the order for a further ten Carthusians to be taken from the London Charterhouse to Newgate prison, chained upright in a filthy cellar and left there to die of starvation. It is said that one of them took five months to die but there is some evidence that Sir Thomas More's daughter persuaded the warders to let her bring them food until suspicion was aroused and it became too dangerous. One lay Brother, William Horne, managed to survive the fate of his fellow monks only to be transferred to the Tower, nursed back to some degree of normal health so that Cromwell could indulge his desire to have him tortured and die a slow lingering death. Eventually, Horne too was killed at Tyburn in 1540, ironically just two weeks after Thomas Cromwell himself had reaped his reward at the block on Tower Hill.

Also in May 1537, two monks from the Charterhouse at Kingston upon Hull had been taken to York to be hung in chains. Monks in other Charterhouses either fled the country or were dispersed. One, Dom Maurice Chauncey, pretended to accept the Act of Supremacy in order to save his Charterhouse, but nevertheless had to flee the country. He bitterly repented the fact that he had not accepted a martyr's fate, and came back after Edward VI's death to re-establish a small Carthusian community at Sheen, which was eventually exiled by Elizabeth. The Carthusians, the most precious jewel of the Catholic Church, were not to return to England until the late nineteenth century.[1]

At the time of the Dissolution of the Monasteries, the way of life of the monks in many of the communities had undoubtedly deteriorated. In consequence, and also through being led astray by the weakness of the bishops, many communities took the easy way out by acknowledging Henry VIII. It was precisely because the Carthusians were known to be steadfast and uncorrupt that Henry VIII and Thomas Cromwell knew they had to be destroyed.

This disgraceful carnage, among the foulest deeds in English history, was but a transient success for the earthly

[1] Only one hundred yards from Marble Arch in London lie the Tyburn shrine and the Benedictine Convent of the Adoration of the Sacred Heart. The sisters pray for the Carthusians every day. In September 1950, in commemoration of the centenary of the official return of the Catholic Church to England, the Prior of Parkminster celebrated mass at the convent, the first Carthusian to offer mass publicly in London since John Houghton had been executed. The same weekend no fewer than seven cardinals visited the Tyburn shrine.

lust and adaptable conscience of a king. The spirit of the Carthusian martyrs will shine down on us from heaven until the end of time.

Accounts of Carthusian martyrdom in other countries can also be told, but I have related the story of the English martyrs at some length so that the reader can appreciate the burning faith with which those in Charterhouses have been and still are infused.

*1. The Great Cloister.
A Carthusian returning from church to his cell.*

*2. Communion at La Grande Chartreuse.*

3. Pope John Paul II and the local diocesan Bishop of Cantanzaro with the Carthusians at La Torre in October 1984, on the eve of St Bruno's Feast Day, when the Pope prayed at St Bruno's tomb.

*4. The chapel, two miles up the mountain
from La Grande Chartreuse, which marks the site
of St Bruno's original foundation in 1084.*

*5a. The church of the Charterhouse of the Transfiguration, Vermont, USA.*

*5b. An aerial view of St Hugh's Charterhouse, Sussex, England.*

*6a. The Charterhouse of
Notre-Dame de Portes,
established in 1115.*

*6b. Carthusians
in their stalls
for Divine Office.*

*7a. A Carthusian nun in the sixteenth-century great cloister
in the Spanish Charterhouse at Benifaça.*

*7b. A Benifaça nun receives the ancient sacrament
of Virginal Consecration, unique to the Carthusians.*

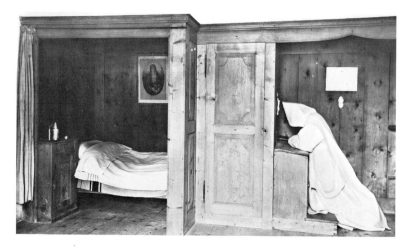

*8a. A Carthusian at prayer in his cell
in the Swiss Charterhouse at Valsainte.*

*8b. At manual work in a cell.*

# VII

# FROM THE REFORMATION TO THE TWENTIETH CENTURY

Boundless, endless and sublime,
The image of eternity.

*Lord Byron, 1788–1824*

Including the English houses, a total of forty-four Charterhouses were suppressed in Europe during the Reformation. Luther's appearance on the religious scene at about the same time that Henry VIII wanted his divorce was a coincidence which made them allies. Despite all the persecutions of the period, or perhaps because they turned good men's hearts towards a better life, vocations for the Carthusian way continued, and in the seventeenth century twenty-one new Charterhouses were established.

Père Charles de Condren (1588–1641), the second superior-general of the Oratorians and very aware of man's insignificance, wrote of the seventeenth-century Carthusians in his posthumously published *Discours et Lettres* of 1643:

> Their duties are confined to singing God's praises day and night, like the angelic choirs. God happily frees them from all dealings with the world, because he wishes them to deal with heaven. Thus, without ceasing, they are lifted out of themselves in the contemplation of divine things. Night falls not upon them since it is during earth's dark hours that they carry on their holy work as Children of Light.

By 1676 the Carthusians had recovered to such an extent that there were no fewer than 173 Charterhouses, containing a total of some 2,300 choir monks, 1,500 lay Brothers and 120 nuns.

Sadly, in the eighteenth century the nationalistic spirit of some rulers who wanted complete control over the Church within their own dominions saw the Republic of Venice and the Emperor Joseph of Austria suppress all their Charterhouses. Tuscany also closed down two houses. When the bloody days of the French Revolution arrived, and all the Church's assets were seized and religious orders dispersed, there were 126 Charterhouses, of which seventy-five were in France. All the French Charterhouses were confiscated and pillaged, and some forty to fifty monks were guillotined or, sent to the galleys like common criminals, died at their oars. Many more were exiled. There were martyrs among the Carthusian nuns as well: the prioress and two sisters of the Gosnay Charterhouse in Picardy were executed, while others died in prison.

The situation deteriorated further during the time of Napoleon when all but five Charterhouses were suppressed, yet following the Bonaparte era Louis XVIII permitted the monks to return to La Grande Chartreuse in 1816 and gradually monasteries were reacquired in Italy and Savoy. Nevertheless, persecution persisted: during the 1834 revolution in Portugal all the Portuguese Charterhouses were suppressed, and in the following year Spain seized all Carthusian properties and dispersed the monks. In Switzerland too, the home of Calvinism, Charterhouses were suppressed.

Towards the end of the nineteenth century the irrepressible Carthusians succeeded in reacquiring monasteries in Germany, Italy, Switzerland and Spain as well as in France. In the 1870s the building of England's first Charterhouse since Tudor times was begun; completed in

1883, St Hugh's, Parkminster, in Sussex, is the largest Charterhouse ever built in England. It came into being as a potential house of refuge and was used as such for a time when the anti-clerical Clemenceau, a lapsed Catholic, exiled the Carthusians from France along with other religious orders in 1901. The monks of La Grande Chartreuse itself went to Farneta in Italy, and although the Carthusians returned to France in 1928, to Montrieux and Selignac, La Grande Chartreuse itself was only regained in 1940 in the confusion of World War II.

At the close of the nineteenth century the Carthusian Order consisted of some seven hundred monks and about one hundred nuns. On 1 December 1983, in twenty-three Charterhouses (seventeen for monks and six for nuns) there were 205 choir monks, 181 Brothers, ninety-five nuns and thirty-nine novices and postulants. Between them, the monks and nuns represented twenty-six different nationalities. Though not great in number they are, in the words of Pope Pius XI, 'the most powerful pleaders with our most merciful God in all Christendom', and it is good to note that in recent years the numbers entering the novitiates have been tending to increase.

A milestone in the history of the order was reached in 1950, with the establishment of the first Charterhouse in the United States, in Vermont; it consisted originally of only four shanties deep in the woods. Postulants presented themselves from time to time and were tested for a few months before being sent to a Charterhouse in Europe for their novitiate. Few were able to endure the fasting and solitude in the frozen silence of a winter in La Grande Chartreuse! But some came through the trial, and from these small beginnings developed an American stronghold of prayer. On the prospects of Carthusians in America, Thomas Merton wrote: 'A Charterhouse in America would have to meet the great temptations that that country offers: publicity, technology, popularity, commercialism, machines. However, one feels that the Carthusians are equipped as no other Order to resist this attack.' Indeed they have done so.

In their life of seclusion and prayer, Carthusians have contributed much to religious literature at the highest spiritual level. Just as St Thomas Aquinas is known as the 'Angelic Doctor', Denis the Carthusian (1402–71) is called the 'Ecstatic Doctor'. Probably the most prolific of all sacred writers, Denis the Carthusian's works consist of no fewer than forty-two stout volumes of some seven hundred pages each; he wrote more than two hundred tracts, of which the most famous is probably *De Contemplatione*, on a wide variety of spiritual topics, some dealing with the most sublime of mysteries. The reader receives the distinct feeling from his writings that they are analogous to the basket-weaving of the Desert Fathers – written as a mere accompaniment to prayer, with no thought of permanence or posterity. Carthusian writers are renowned for their writings on mystical themes, and the *Dictionary of Ascetic and Mystical Spirituality*, compiled by Dom Yves Gourdel, contains sixteen whole columns of them.[1]

The bulk of Carthusian writings dealing, as they do, largely with mystical experiences, are of necessity esoteric. Perhaps the best definition of such writing is provided by the late Dom John Chapman (1865–1933), Abbot of Downside, when he described it as 'the direct secret and incommunicable knowledge of God received in contemplation'. Put in another way, much of these Carthusian

---

[1] Although Walter Hilton (died *c.* 1400), the author of *The Ladder of Perfection* was undoubtedly very close to the Carthusians and much respected by the order, claims that he was a Carthusian remain as unsubstantiated as the suggestion that it was he who wrote *The Cloud of Unknowing*.

writings, holy as they are, are attempts to communicate that which cannot be communicated except to others who have also had mystical experiences.

Of the other many important books to emerge from Charterhouses, undoubtedly one of the greatest was *The Life of Christ* by Ludolph of Saxony (1295–1377). This book was a special favourite of St Teresa of Avila and played a large part in the conversion of St Ignatius of Loyola.

Inspired spiritual advice is timeless, eternal, but some doubting Thomases may seek a twentieth-century Desert Father for guidance. They need look no further than the pages of some quite remarkable little books by the Carthusian Augustin Guillerand (1877–1945). In his total humility he was concerned so little with this world that he destroyed most of his writings. Fortunately some were saved and edited after his death: *They Speak by Silences* and *Where Silence Is Praise* have brought solace, peace and ultimate wisdom to many thousands of people. Father Guillerand's books were originally published as being 'By a Carthusian Monk', in conformity with the Carthusian tenet of self-effacement. The identity of Carthusian authors is only revealed after they have been dead some time – and not always then.

When it comes to saints, I must refer again to the old Carthusian adage: 'To make saints, not to publicise them.' Because of the Carthusian Order's refusal to put forward its members for canonisation, and because those in Charterhouses live out their lives in seclusion, there are relatively few formally recognised Carthusian saints. (The word 'saint' comes from the Latin *sanctus*, which means 'holy man'. When the Catholic Church, after due consideration, declares someone to be a saint, what it is really saying is that it is certain that the man or woman concerned is in heaven. Everyone in heaven is a saint.) Apart from St Bruno himself, other Carthusian saints include St

Hugh of Lincoln – the only Carthusian to become an English bishop and the very first Carthusian to be canonised, St Anthelme, who instituted the first General Chapter of the Carthusians in 1140, St Artaud and St Roseline.

To the extent that everyone in a Charterhouse is 'holy', in God's eyes they are all saintly. Miracles are not the only proof of sanctity, but again, to the extent that they are, I have heard of a number of 'miraculous' happenings inside Charterhouses. Many of these, and ancillary mystical experiences, are recorded in the archives of the Order – in particular in *Les Annales* and in *Les Ephémérides*; others have never been chronicled, nor are they likely to be.[1]

There exists a probably apocryphal but totally symbolic story of the Carthusian monk whose duty it was regularly to visit a village close to his monastery to fetch water for his brethren from a well. The villagers began to notice that whenever the monk went to the well somebody very ill was immediately cured. Soon the sick for many miles around were brought to the well for the monk to heal when he came to fetch water. Eventually, the news of what was happening got to the ears of the prior of the monastery. He sent for the monk concerned: 'What's all this I hear about you performing miracles in the village? It's got to stop. Except for essential duties, the business of all good Carthusians is to be in their cells praying to God!'

Throughout their history, the Carthusians have been a prime source of inspiration to many saints including St Dominic, St Teresa of Avila and St Thomas More, who tested his vocation at the London Charterhouse in his youth. It was Carthusian perfection which brought about the conversion of St Ignatius of Loyola; St Ignatius and St

---

[1] The carefully preserved and largely concealed archives of the Carthusian Order are said to be the most comprehensive of any religious order in the world. The question poses itself: should these be made available to bona-fide historians, or do they belong more to heaven than to earth?

Francis Xavier, both of whom considered joining the Carthusians, affiliated their own order – the Jesuits – to them, almost as soon as it was established, in community of prayer and sacrifice.

Ever targets for persecution, the Carthusians have served God by emulating, to the highest degree of which man is capable, the life of Christ himself. Their fidelity to their unchanged ideal has been astonishing. Through the power of their prayer and their steadfast holding to the supernatural life, they exert a truly eternal influence on Church and man. In the words of Archbishop Goudier: 'A more humiliating record of the so-called progress of the world could scarcely be written than that of the Carthusian monasteries in Europe. In them, strikingly, the prophesy of the second Chapter of the Book of Wisdom[1] is fulfilled.'

The Order has had to contend with the Black Death, which claimed some nine hundred victims, avalanches, fires, the Reformation, the French Revolution, the various attempts throughout history to suppress it, and two world wars. Yet today, twentieth-century Carthusians continue to be the main beacons of prayer in the world to inspire popes, bishops, priests and all mankind. Living day and night with God, they are changeless, living examples to us all.

---

[1] The Book of Wisdom tells of the hatred of the sinner for the virtuous, and Christian tradition understands it as forecasting the Passion of Christ. Chapter II expands the philosophy of the godless, and relates their hostility to people of virtue which they see as a reproach to their own self-indulgent, materialistic lives.

# VIII

# LIFE IN A CHARTERHOUSE: THE FATHERS

Battering the gates of Heaven with stones of prayer.

*Alfred, Lord Tennyson, 1809–92*

In their essentials, today's Charterhouses differ little from those of St Bruno's time. The buildings may be more solid, meals cooked by electricity or gas, and modern fertilisers used in the growing of vegetables, but a Charterhouse remains, as in the eleventh century, a sanctuary for those seeking to live with, for and in God alone. In their cells, grouped around a central church, the Carthusians live in silence and solitude.

Those entering Charterhouses, be they priest or layman, are first and foremost drawn to the Carthusian way. Whether a layman joining the order may find he has, additionally, a calling to become a Choir Monk and priest is something he will find out once he has entered a Charterhouse.

In years gone by the Carthusian Fathers, that is to say ordained monks, were men of education, whereas the Brothers, or unordained monks, although dedicated to Carthusian life, were in the main uneducated and concentrated on attending to the material needs of the community. With the spread of education, an increasing number of newcomers to the Order, although scholarly and well qualified to study for priesthood, now opt for a Brother's vocation on the grounds that ordination is not a prerequisite for attaining the highest peaks of spirituality. Indeed there are some who consider that priesthood could be a hindrance, such as being psychologically associated with privilege or spiritual pride; they point to their fore-fathers in the Egyptian desert, the majority of whom were not ordained.

Today, although the vocational requirements are different, Fathers and Brothers form a closely knit com-munity. Yet, because their lives do differ in a number of respects, I shall examine the lives of each category sep-arately.

The 'cell' in which a Father passes most of his life is really a little cottage-hermitage on two floors. Entered by a door off the cloisters, it is built in such a way that none of its windows overlooks any other hermitage. Once in his cell, the Carthusian Father's solitude is total, and in many ways greater than that of the recluses of earlier centuries. Not for nothing are the words 'Our conversation is in Heaven' inscribed over many cell doors.

The Carthusian's cell is his Bethlehem, where he starts a new life, and his Nazareth, where he abides in silence and obscurity. It is also his Calvary, where obedience never ceases to offer him sacrifice on the cross. It is where God and his servant commune together.

Downstairs is the wood store for his fire in the winter, and next to it a room with a carpenter's bench and wood-working tools. The Carthusian does not forget that Christ was a carpenter. Downstairs, too, he has a little walled-in garden which he tends, unseen by all.

Up a short flight of stairs are the Father's living quarters. Here he has a small ante-chamber for use as a work room which includes a statue of the Virgin Mary before which, whenever he enters his cell, he recites an Ave Maria. The ante-room leads into the cell proper (or cubiculum); this is simultaneously his bedroom, his refectory and his study. At one end small doors give access to a little washroom and a lavatory. The furniture is as simple as can be – table, chair, prie-dieu, bed with straw mattress, woollen coverlets and a chaff pillow, and a wood-burning stove. If heaven contained houses, I am sure the rooms in them would be much like those of the Carthusian monks.

The Carthusian day begins at an hour when much of the world is carousing or just starting to sleep off the excesses of a materialistic day. At 11.45 p.m. the monk rises from his austere bed to say the Little Office of Our Lady, then, leaving his cell, he wends his way through the cloisters to the monastery church. The choir stalls fill up, the professed monks in their white habits, the Novices in their black cloaks. The church is in almost total darkness, the only light coming from the sanctuary lamp and the shaded low lamps in the choir. After a period of deep silence the chanting of the long night vigil of Matins and Lauds begins. The chanting carries, in its cadences, soaring praises of God, then sinks down to lowly supplication. At times it almost seems to break into a sobbing of repentance before pouring itself out in heartfelt whispers of love. The singing, steeped in Gregorian antiquity,[1] has a holiness all its own, and as a sung office proceeds it is impossible not to sense how the fervour of the Psalms takes over, enveloping not only the monks but also the listener in the tribune.[2]

The purity of the Carthusian chant – *viva et rotunda voce* – has been jealously maintained for centuries; slower, lower-pitched and less melismatic than the Benedictine chant, it is considered more deeply spiritual by those who have heard both. The seventeenth-century Cardinal Bona, who undertook vast research into liturgy, records that it was the Carthusian chant which Christ recommended in his revelations to St Bridget, the patron saint of

[1] There is a twelfth-century gradual at the Parkminster Charterhouse which may have been used by St Bruno himself.
[2] The gallery in the Church used to accommodate any visitors fortunate enough to penetrate a Charterhouse.

Sweden. No organ or other musical instrument accompanies the chant, and in his liturgy the Carthusian seems to be projected by its sacred power to a point where eternity meets his temporal existence.[1]

This great night vigil of Matins and Lauds, in which Carthusian prayer brings heaven down towards earth and lifts earth towards heaven, lasts some two to three hours. Matins consists of several 'nocturns', each of which usually contains six Psalms (or some Canticles) and in the course of the night office there will be a reading from the Gospel. Normally in the course of each week all 150 Psalms will be sung.

The night vigil over, some time between 2.30 and 3 a.m. the Father returns to his cell to sleep until 6.45 a.m., when he rises once more to recite in his cell the Little Office of Our Lady. This is followed, again in cell, by the ancient office of Prime, which consists of three Psalms, the creed, a hymn and some readings. The two offices together will occupy him some twenty-five minutes.

Prime over, from about 7.15 a.m. the Carthusian Father spends the next three-quarters of an hour in private prayer. At 8 a.m. the Little Office of Our Lady is said again, followed by the office of Terce which, with its three Psalms, is very similar to Prime.

At 8.15 a.m. the monk leaves his cell for the second time to attend a conventual (i.e. communal) Mass in the monastery church. (The taking of communion is optional at the mass, since all the fathers say their own individual Masses in small private chapels in the course of the day, at a time normally of their own choosing.)

The Carthusian Mass, devoid of pomp and needless ceremonial, closely resembles the old rite which Charlemagne obtained from Rome in the eighth century and has been little changed in a thousand years. Shorter than the

---

[1] Even Benedictines, renowned for their singing, with whom I have spoken admit to the greater spirituality of the Carthusian chant.

Tridentine and modern rites, it is of beautiful simplicity. As an act of humility and thanksgiving, the Carthusian will spend a time prostrate on the ground during Mass, be it a conventual or an individual Mass.[1]

Following Mass and until 11.15 a.m. the Carthusian Father devotes himself in his cell to spiritual exercises, prayer, reading and absorbing the Scriptures in *lectio divina*. No special methods of prayer are laid down: each monk is free to follow the path from which he expects to reap most fruit. At 11.15 a.m., still in cell, the Little Office of Our Lady is again recited before the office of Sext, which is very similar to that of Prime and Terce.

Then, at 11.30 a.m., having had nothing to eat or drink since 5 p.m. the day before, the Carthusian Father has dinner. It is brought to him in a 'gamelle' – a kind of billycan – by a Brother and passed to him through a hatch in the wall of his cell. Reading, perhaps one of the lives of the Desert Fathers, he will eat slowly, finishing at about 12.30 p.m. Until 1.15 p.m. his time is his own in which to relax or do some work in his cell: cleaning it, perhaps doing some washing, or mending.

At 1.15 p.m. the church bell peals, as it has for all the other offices – to announce Nones. Similar to the offices of Prime, Terce and Sext, it too is said alone in cell – again preceded by the Little Office of Our Lady.

For the next two hours, until 3.30 p.m. the father remains in his cell studying, praying privately and perhaps attending to his small garden or undertaking some woodwork. Before Vespers, at 3.45 p.m., when he goes to meet his brethren in church for the third and last time of his day, the Little Office of Our Lady is recited yet again.

When the great church bell peals out the call for Vespers, as each monk enters the church he takes a brief turn

[1] Most – though not all – Charterhouses have a chapel attached, with access from outside the monastery, where on Sundays one of the Carthusian fathers will celebrate mass at which the general public may assist.

on the bell rope before proceeding to his place in the choir stalls facing the massive, beautiful and ancient choir books. So large and clear are both words and music that each book can be readily shared by three monks. Vespers, which includes four Psalms, a hymn, and the Salve Regina, lasts about half an hour.

On returning to his cell after Vespers, the Carthusian Father spends half an hour in prayer, reading and studying before his supper, which is brought to him by a Brother at 4.45 p.m. After supper he will spend about another two and a half hours in spiritual exercises.

The last Angelus[1] of the day is tolled at 6.45 p.m. Some time between then and 7.30 p.m. the Carthusian, still in his cell, says his Compline, followed by the office of Compline of Our Lady, each of which includes three Psalms.

And so to bed at about 8 p.m. in his hair shirt on his straw mattress. It has been an intensely busy day: busy with intense prayer and busy with tranquil activity. Time seems to be at a premium in a Charterhouse; the only complaint of the monks is that there are insufficient hours in the day to fit in all the prayer they would like. In fact, after eliminating time spent sleeping, eating, tending to his cell and doing a little manual work, the Carthusian Father spends some fourteen hours a day in prayer, *lectio divina* and study, six of these hours in church and eight alone in his cell.

---

[1] The call to prayer to commemorate the Incarnation, made at sunrise, noon and sunset. The Carthusians have a fourth Angelus during the night after the Night Office of Matins and Lauds.

# IX

# LIFE IN A CHARTERHOUSE:
## THE BROTHERS

We were brothers all,
In honour as in one community.

*William Wordsworth, 1770–1850*

From the earliest days the Carthusians had lay Brothers to provide services and craft work for the monastery as a whole. For many years the lay Brothers lived in a separate establishment lower down the mountain at La Grande Chartreuse, and separate dwelling houses for the Brothers was the custom at a number of other Charterhouses, including several in England before the Reformation.

Today, as I have already explained, the lives of Fathers and Brothers are much more closely integrated: *all* are monks. The Brothers live within the monasteries in cells which until recently were smaller than those of the Fathers – single rooms, in fact – but the present trend in the Order is for Brothers to occupy hermitages similar to those of the Fathers if they so wish and if spare cells of this type are available.

As opposed to the Fathers, the Brothers spend much of their time out of their cells, attending to the vital business of keeping the monastery running. Food has to be prepared and cooked, the vegetable garden and orchard tended, grass cut, trees felled for firewood, a plumbing job dealt with, some paintwork to be done, a sick monk cared for in his cell, a tile on a roof replaced. The Brothers' jobs are endless. In all these matters it is the aim of a Charterhouse to fend for itself.

Much of the spiritual life of the Brothers – hours of offices, mealtimes, sleeping time and so on is the same as for the Fathers. This chapter concentrates on the differences.

A Brother will spend up to seven hours a day on his particular duties, which are termed obediences. These are allocated to him by the Procurator,[1] normally according to the Brother's natural abilities – the crafts he may have brought with him into the monastery or those he has acquired within it. Sometimes he will have more than one skill, and be both cook and bricklayer, for instance.

Clearly, because of his duties the Carthusian Brother is unable to spend as much time in his cell in prayer as does the Father, nor need he spend quite so much time on the offices and in church. Nevertheless he devotes his whole day's work to God and his monastery which is, for him, God's dwelling place. He will pray silently within his heart while at his work, which is so arranged that it is almost always carried out in solitude and, for the most part, in silence.

It is obligatory for a Brother to attend Matins – the first half of the night vigil – each day and also Mass and Vespers on Sundays and solemn feast days. On other days attendance at Mass, Lauds – the second half of the night vigil – and Vespers is optional, but provided their work permits, the Brothers will participate in as many of the optional offices as possible.

Like the Fathers, Brothers normally have dinner in their cells at 11.30 a.m. and are always in their cells from 6.45 p.m. until the start of the night vigil. They keep abstinence and fast as do the Fathers, although Brothers involved in heavy manual work may have breakfast.

---

[1] For details of the office of procurator see page 99.

[59]

Every year, each Brother makes a 'retreat' from his obediences and remains in the peace and solitude of his cell for eight days – which may be either eight consecutive days, or divided into two periods of a few days each. On Sundays and solemn feast days, and one further day per month if he so wishes, a Brother will remain in his cell for most of the day in recollection.[1]

Although not an ordained priest, a Carthusian Brother is just as much a monk as any of the Fathers and takes the same vows as the Choir Monks. As mentioned earlier, in the days of the Desert Fathers the great majority of monks were not ordained. Monks who are priests will always be necessary in monasteries for the celebration of Mass, if for no other reason, but it is not essential to be a priest in order to become a monk.

Some relevant passages from the Carthusian Statutes will help to explain both the similarities and the differences between the Brothers' vocation and that of the Fathers:

> They [the Brothers] imitate the hidden life of Jesus at Nazareth when carrying out the daily tasks of the house. They praise God by their work. The Fathers, by the very fact of faithful observance of solitude, impart to the Charterhouse its special character and they give spiritual aid to the Brothers from whom in turn they receive much. . . .
>
> Whenever the Brothers are not occupied with the Divine Office in Church or with work in their Obediences, they always return to cell as to a very sure and tranquil haven. Here they remain quietly and without noise as far as possible and follow with faithfulness the Order of the day, doing everything in the presence of God and in the name of Our Lord Jesus Christ, through him giving thanks to God the Father. Here they occupy themselves

[1] 'Recollection' is a term frequently used in the monastic world, and denotes the expulsion from the mind of all distracting thoughts and the collecting together and concentration of one's entire thoughts on prayer.

usefully in reading or meditation, especially on sacred scripture, the food of the soul, or, in the measure possible, they give themselves to prayer. . . .

Interior recollection during work will lead a Brother to contemplation. To attain this recollection it is always permissible while working to have recourse to short and, so to speak, ejaculatory prayers and even sometimes to interrupt the work with brief prayer. . . .

The aim of a Brother's life is above all else that he be united with Christ and that he may abide in his love. Hence, whether in the solitude of his cell or in the midst of his work, aided by the grace of his vocation, he should strive wholeheartedly and at all times to keep his mind on God.

Apart from fully professed Brothers, known as converse Brothers, a Charterhouse may contain one or two donate Brothers whose lives are similar in every way to that of the converse Brothers, and who wear the same habits as the other monks, but who take no solemn vows. They 'donate' or promise their lives to the service of the order, either on a temporary basis or for life.

A certain elasticity is applied to Donates to enable individuals to concentrate on those particular aspects of the Carthusian vocation to which they are most suited. In some cases it is a means of accommodating into the unique religious life of the Carthusians certain exceptional personalities who, for psychological reasons perhaps, may feel unable to take the irrevocable step of renouncing the world for ever through monastic vows. Usually these special cases spend their whole lives in Charterhouses just as if they had taken vows. A Donate is a full member of the order, and as the Carthusian Statutes state: 'Quite frequently, in fact, men of real holiness, who wished to be numbered among the sons of blessed Bruno and to enjoy his heritage have preferred to live and die as Donates.'

More rarely one may find in a Charterhouse a man

[61]

known as a familiar. He will live in the monastery and lead a semi-monastic life, but wear ordinary clothes and carry out duties similar to those of a domestic. A familiar is usually a man who has felt a call to the Carthusian way but has found that his health or temperament cannot stand the full rigours of Carthusian life.

# X

# THE CARTHUSIAN NUNS

Fair Sister of the Seraphim!

*Richard Crashaw, 1612–49*

To most people the word 'nun' probably conjures up the image of a devout woman devoting her life to the sick and the aged or teaching in a convent school. My own admiration for nuns dates from the tender age of seven when I had my appendix removed in a French hospital staffed by nuns. I do not forget the loving kindness I received at their hands.

Yet, just as there are monks given wholly to contemplation, so also are there contemplative nuns: their vocation is almost as old as that of monks. Indeed, St Jerome established a community of nuns in the desert, and St Antony's sister became a nun in 270. Carthusians are in the forefront of today's contemplative nuns but, in their hidden life, they are clearly very much less in evidence than their sisters out in the world.

The first Carthusian monastery for nuns – the Order does not refer to 'convents' – was established at Prebayon in the wild, lonely, narrow valley of Trignion in Provence in 1147, only forty-six years after the death of St Bruno. The founders were a small group of nuns, originally of the Rule of St Caesarius of Arles (469–542), who pined for a deeper interior life than that provided by cenobitism. For guidance towards building a contemplative life they turned to Blessed John of Spain, Prior of Montrieux – one of the earliest Charterhouses – who provided them with a copy of Guiges' *Consuetudines* and details of the Carthusian liturgy. Within the next fifty years or so some six more houses of nuns became affiliated to the Carthusians, and the Statutes[1] of the order produced in 1259 devoted two chapters to the nuns.

That the nuns of the Carthusian Order have never been as numerous as the monks is partly due to the great degree of physical austerity demanded by the order, and partly for financial reasons. Fewer benefactors have come forward for the nuns' Charterhouses, and in former times many people who did contribute money or property had the ulterior motive of wanting to 'buy' places for their younger and unmarriageable daughters. Such corruptive attempts were particularly prevalent during the fourteenth century, although quickly stamped on by the General Chapter[2] and by the visitors. Charterhouses were forbidden to accept money from the families of nuns, and from 1600 La Grande Chartreuse undertook to provide financial support for the nuns when necessary.

Spiritually at one with the monks of the Order, and equally dedicated to a life of silent contemplation, the nuns enjoyed rather less solitude in the early years of the Order. Unable to afford the cost of building individual cells, they slept in dormitories and ate together – yet in silence – in refectories.

Although subject to regular 'Visitations' from the thirteenth century onwards by a Carthusian Prior to ensure that the nuns were abiding by the basic rules of the Order, the Prioresses originally had considerable independence and authority. Coincidental with the introduction of visitations, a Carthusian Father was detached to celebrate mass and to take over the spiritual welfare of each Char-

---

[1] From 1690 the nuns effectively had Statutes of their own.
[2] For an explanation of the functions of the General Chapter and of visitors see Chapter XV.

terhouse of nuns. Living in a separate house attached to, but outside, the nuns' enclosures, the Vicar, as he is called, has acted as spiritual director to the nuns ever since. To help him, he has another Father (or co-adjutor) and one or two Brothers to tend to the vicariate and, perhaps, work on the land.

Over the centuries the number of Carthusian monasteries for nuns has fluctuated; a peak of seven houses with two affiliated houses was reached in the thirteenth century. Just as the Carthusian monks have suffered many persecutions in their history, so have the nuns. At different times their houses have been suppressed and the nuns dispersed, many having to flee to other countries. The Prioress of the Gosnay Charterhouse in northern France, along with two sisters, was, as I have mentioned earlier, guillotined during the French Revolution, while others died in prison.

In 1794 not one house of Carthusian nuns remained, but after the defeat of Napoleon several dispersed sisters came together to reopen, in 1822, a monastery at Beauregard in France. This was to be the only Charterhouse allowed to remain in France when Clemenceau expelled the religious orders. Although Beauregard was disgracefully invaded and ransacked by French mounted police, the nuns would not be moved, and eventually a state decision of 1907 permitted purely contemplative nuns to remain *in situ*. Sadly, because of urbanisation and the threat of a motorway the historic house of Beauregard was closed in 1973. A replacement monastery for the nuns was built at Reillane in the Alpes Maritimes in Haute-Provence. Until the twentieth century almost all the nuns' monasteries had been established either in France or in Italy, but in 1967 the now thriving Spanish Charterhouse of Benifaça (Valencia) was opened.

The difference between Carthusian Fathers and Brothers is paralleled in the nuns' houses by Choir Nuns and Lay Sisters. All are called 'Sister' with the exception of the prioress and her deputy, the Sub-prioress, who are called 'Mother'.

A day in the life of a Choir Nun is very similar to that of a Carthusian Father, except that she cannot celebrate Mass. She says the same offices, passes the same long night vigil, and spends as much time on spiritual exercises. In some houses she eats with the other nuns at midday, but alone in her cell in the evening; however the present trend among the Carthusian nuns is towards greater solitude, and in some Charterhouses the nuns eat together only on Sundays and religious feast days. A Choir Nun may undertake a little manual work to help the running of her house, but most of it is done by the Lay Sisters.

Until relatively recently the cells of Choir Nuns were merely single rooms, but the post-war Benifaca Charterhouse provides small hermitages with individual gardens. This is also true of both the Riva and Vedana nuns' Charterhouses in Italy.

The rules relating to abstinence and fasting are substantially the same as those for the monks, and up to three times a week the nuns have 'recreation' when they spend an hour walking and talking together. At those houses where hermitages exist, a weekly spatiamentum (walk) for Choir Nuns is arranged instead.

Mass is celebrated daily by the Vicar or his deputy in a chapel which straddles, so to speak, the monastery walls. An iron grille divides the chapel in half, with the celebrant of the Mass one side and the nuns on the other. Communion is given through a small opening in the centre of the grille.

Generally speaking, no man is ever allowed inside the nuns' monasteries – not even the visitor or the Vicar – except for the annual visit by the local bishop and, on occasions, when the Brothers in the vicariate enter the grounds to undertake some of the heavier agricultural work. One room in the vicariate is designated as the parlour, and here the Vicar may have discussions with the Prioress or other visitors. Members of the rest of the community will only talk to the Vicar in the confessional, one side of which is in the vicariate and the other in the monastery.

Administration of a Charterhouse for nuns is vested in the Prioress, assisted by the Prioress' Council, which consists of two nuns elected by the community and two nuns nominated by the Prioress, who is herself elected by the whole community.

A guest house is attached to each Charterhouse. Here both male and female relatives of every nun may stay and visit for two days each year.

Life for the Lay Sisters is broadly similar to that of Carthusian Brothers: they attend to the cooking, cleaning, laundry, gardening and so on. Yet, like the Brothers, they spend much time in prayer and like them attend the same communal offices. Both Choir Nuns and Lay Sisters wear the same habit: white with a black veil.

Anyone wishing to become a Carthusian Choir Nun must be at least twenty and not more than thirty-five. She will spend six months as a Postulant, two years in the Novitiate, and a further two years as a Donate with temporary vows. After five and a half years, and being at least twenty-five years old, she will make her perpetual vows which are the same as those of the monks. The probationary period for Lay Sisters and permanent Donates is approximately the same.

After solemn profession of her vows a Carthusian Choir Nun subsequently goes through the unique and ancient privilege of Virginal Consecration. This ceremony, conducted by a bishop, descends from the ancient rite of deaconess in the early Christian Church, and has been a practice among Carthusian nuns since the twelfth century. Recently Virginal Consecration has been made available to

Lay Sisters, although it is not obligatory for them. All Carthusian nuns take on the additional name of Mary once they have been fully accepted into the order.

A Carthusian Choir Nun is entitled to read the Gospel at Matins. For this she wears a stole, as she also does when distributing communion in the absence of a priest.

The Carthusian principle of making saints but not publicising them applies just as much to the nuns as it does to the monks. The nuns' Charterhouses have produced countless holy souls, most of them unknown to this world but all surely very close to God in the next. St Roseline (1263–1329) is one of the better-known Carthusian saints: a member of the aristocratic de Villeneuve family, she became Abbess of the Celle-Ronbaud Charterhouse and was canonised in 1851. Many beautiful writings by Carthusian nuns are preserved in La Grande Chartreuse; those of Margaret, Prioress of Ornacieux (died 1310), describing some of her mystical visions, are especially noteworthy, as are some fine mystical writings of the nun Anne Griffen (died 1641).

Like the monks, Carthusian nuns come from many different countries and walks of life. Among them are former teachers, lawyers, artists, peasants and women of noble birth.

# XI

# WHO JOINS THE CARTHUSIANS AND HOW

God does not reserve such a lofty vocation [that of mystical contemplation] to certain souls only; on the contrary he is willing that all should embrace it.

*St John of the Cross, 1542–91*

Whenever people question me about Carthusians, their first queries usually relate to the kind of existence lived in a Charterhouse. Almost invariably, however, probing questions follow about the type of person who joins the Carthusians and how he or she goes about it.

Such curiosity frequently reflects genuine puzzlement that anyone could know whether or not he had a Carthusian vocation when the order erects so many barriers, seemingly to prevent people finding out anything about life in a Charterhouse. Such barriers are there only to protect the Carthusians from the frivolous or idly curious; they soon come down for anyone who seriously thinks he may have a Carthusian vocation.

Carthusians are drawn from all walks of life. In a Charterhouse, former secular priests or religious of other orders are the exception rather than the rule; you will find former colonels, solicitors, doctors, businessmen, singers, shepherds, waiters, gardeners and the man next door to you, all bound together in their common love for God before all else. An ex-missionary, when asked what he did in his cell, replied: 'I am still a missionary. Formerly I was

[69]

only a missionary in a circumvented area, now through prayer the whole world lies open.'

Carthusian monks I have come to know include Brother Stefan,[1] the son of a Polish railway worker whose family was split up and sent to Siberia when he was a child, after the Russians occupied his home town in World War I. As a teenager he escaped during the Russian Revolution, only to become a prisoner of the Germans. The war over, Stefan, brought up in the Orthodox faith, converted to Catholicism. Later he joined the Polish Army and married, but tragically his wife, who worked for the Polish Underground during World War II, was killed by the Gestapo. Stefan succeeded in getting out of Poland to reach the West and join the Polish forces fighting alongside the Allies. Following the Normandy landings, Stefan visited the shrine of St Thérèse at Lisieux, where he felt a call to join a religious order. The war over, on the suggestion of a Polish priest he undertook retreats with the Benedictines and also in a Charterhouse. He has never had any doubts that he made the right choice by opting for the Carthusian vocation. His sparkling eyes aglow with happiness, he once said to me, 'If God did not want me to be here, I would not be here!'

A very different type of Carthusian whom I have met is Father Mark, who comes from an old-established Catholic family and received a good Catholic education. At the unusually early age of twelve Mark decided to become a barrister when he was older. However, the outbreak of World War II when he was sixteen turned him more towards God and belief that perhaps God wanted him to join the Carthusians, of whom he had first heard at the age of ten. Plans to study law at Oxford were abandoned and, after a 'trial' at Parkminster, Mark was found acceptable to the Carthusians. Yet since the war was still in progress he

---

[1] 'Stefan' is a pseudonym, as are the names of other living Carthusians I mention, but their stories are perfectly true.

first joined the Royal Navy and, as a petty officer radar mechanic, saw service afloat in the Mediterranean and in the Far East where he took part in the invasion of the Philippines. On his periodic home leaves, he was able to spend the occasional weekend at Parkminster. Demobilised in 1945, Mark spent a month at home with his family before entering Parkminster for life. Like every Carthusian I have met he has never had even a momentary doubt about his vocation; his happiness, he tells me, has grown as year by year his knowledge and experience of God have increased. Mark has held a number of offices in his Charterhouse and has been on official business to La Grande Chartreuse and also to the United States to help with the establishment of the first American Carthusian monastery.

My good friend Brother Thomas, like Father Mark, also spent World War II at sea, joining the Merchant Navy as a radio officer at the age of seventeen. When peace was declared, Thomas studied electrical engineering before joining a company which supplied specialised equipment to the railways. Business prospered and, although a born and still practising Catholic, Thomas seemed to enjoy what are popularly known as 'the good things in life'. His principal pleasures were hunting, beer and women – in that order, according to his mother – until he began to wonder whether perhaps life held something more than materialism and self-indulgence. As a result he made a retreat in a Benedictine abbey. 'This is the life for me,' thought Thomas, but it was not until three years later that he decided he had been wasting his life in business and on hedonistic pleasure, and joined the Benedictines as a brother. He felt no call to become a priest, but after two or three years in the Benedictine Order sensed the need for a more enclosed and stricter life. It took him a further nine years before taking the second major decision in his life and joining the Carthusians. 'God took me by the scruff of the neck and put me here,' Thomas told me. 'And here I rejoice that my whole life is prayer.'

Another Polish Carthusian I have met is Father Basil. A Catholic born in Warsaw, he had an amazingly varied career before entering a Charterhouse: a student of economics, a teacher, an MP in the first Polish parliament, a diplomat in the Polish Legation in Berlin in Hitler's Germany, and a lieutenant in the Polish Brigade with the French military forces which took part in the Narvik expedition. When France fell he found his way to Britain and joined the Polish Ministry of Foreign Affairs in exile. Until he met the Carthusians he was not a particularly devout Catholic, and the story of how he came to enter a Charterhouse is quite remarkable. During World War II he had once flown over Parkminster, and soon after peace had been declared Basil had an urge to visit out of sheer curiosity the impressive monastery he had seen from the air. A Polish chaplain effected an introduction that enabled Basil to make a brief conducted tour one afternoon. It was midwinter, snow lay on the ground and the sun had already set, but when the Father showing Basil round opened the door to a dark cell and said to him: 'How would you like to spend thirty years here?' a strange metamorphosis came over Basil and he suddenly thought to himself, 'Why not!' Within three months he had made his decision to join the Order, and after his novitiate was ordained as a Choir Monk. He has enjoyed to the full that happiness known only to those who are married to God for life. I asked him once whether, to start with at least, he did not find the rigours of Carthusian life irksome. His face alight with contented good humour, he replied: 'Never. After my experiences in the war, this is like a comfortable hotel!'

From a more conventional background, another Carthusian monk whom I have come to know well is Father Joseph. Born in Dublin of devout Irish Catholic parents, with three uncles in holy orders, he decided on a medical career and took his first degree in medicine at University College, Dublin. Although he had had no thoughts of becoming a religious in his youth, as a young lad of fourteen Joseph had been impressed by a book which he had happened to notice on a secondhand book-stall. It was called *The Contemplative Life, by a Carthusian*, and had a frontispiece of St Bruno at prayer. This attrac-tion to the Carthusian way was revived at university when he came across another book about the order while brows-ing in the library. But Hitler's war created a shortage of doctors in England, and Joseph, by then qualified, spent the next five years working in England and Wales, although all the time aware of his underlying urge to become a Carthusian. Finding himself falling in love, with the possibility of marriage in the offing, a final decision had to be made. To help him reach a conclusion he made a retreat with the Jesuits and decided to join the Carthusians if they would have him. It was not to be – yet. A Jesuit priest persuaded Joseph he would do better to become a Cistercian; he did so, and in time was ordained priest.

Although the Cistercian Joseph was content with his lot, the yearning for the more secluded Carthusian life was never far from his thoughts. Finally, after twelve years, he sought and obtained permission to leave the Cistercians and was accepted as a Carthusian novice. As he walked up the drive to the Charterhouse which was to become his new home, he thought: 'I'll never see Ireland again but here, I know, all my dreams will come true.' On entering the monastery almost the first thing he saw was the original painting of St Bruno, a reproduction of which had been in the book he had seen one day as a fourteen-year-old boy. Later, Father Joseph came to hold more than one official position in his Charterhouse.

I hope that these brief pen portraits of just a few of the Carthusians I have come to know demonstrate clearly that those who join the order are far from being of a type cast in the same mould. Others I have met include a colonel from the French Army, a young monk whose family own a chain of cinemas, a jockey, an international lawyer, an Indian teacher, the son of a docker and a fascinatingly joyous nun who started life as a lawyer. The varied backgrounds are only likely to be matched in the Foreign Legion!

On a number of occasions good men of sincere devotion have told me of the written approaches they have made to a Charterhouse with a view to making retreats in the guest house, only to be told: 'We do not normally accept retreatants unless they wish to make a serious test of the Carthusian vocation.' This may sound a little off-putting, but for a hermitic community detaching itself from this world in order to place God before all else, the regular intrusion of retreatants would clearly erode its solitary way of life.

Anyone seriously drawn to a contemplative life is sure to talk it over with a priest eventually, delve into monastic literature and at least get a rough idea of whether he might – or might not – have a vocation for the Carthusian life. If he feels he would like to test himself for the vocation, or talk it over with the Carthusians themselves, he should write to the Prior of the nearest Charterhouse – which might even be in a country other than his own.

An invitation to spend a few days in the monastery guest house will be extended to a serious applicant, who will then learn something of Carthusian life. He will be interviewed by the Prior and the Novice Master, who will consider his suitability for acceptance on trial as a Postulant.

Assuming that he is considered potentially suitable to be a Choir Monk, the would-be Carthusian Father first spends three months as a Postulant, living more or less the life of a monk but without having professed any kind of vows. If after those three months he still feels he has a Carthusian vocation and is thought to be suitable, the Postulant becomes a Novice. The minimum period of

Novitiate is two years, although this can be extended for a further six months at the Prior's discretion.

A Novice wears a black cloak over a white Carthusian habit, with a shorter cowl than the professed monks. On completion of his novitiate, if still a suitable candidate for the order, he becomes a junior professed monk, which involves taking of simple vows[1] for a three-year period. He now wears the full Carthusian habit.

When the three years are up, all the solemn professed members of the community in his Charterhouse – Fathers and Brothers – vote on his suitability for acceptance into the Order. Two decisions can be reached at such a vote. The junior professed monk can be:

1. Rejected as unsuitable and asked to leave the monastery.

2. Asked to renew his simple vows for a period of a further two years, but while continuing to be a junior professed monk will move out of that part of the monastery where the junior professed monks, Novices and Postulants live to the part where the professed Fathers have their cells.

After a total of about seven and a half years[2] (the approximately two and a half years spent as a Postulant and Novice, and the five years spent as a junior professed monk) the whole community takes a final vote on whether or not to accept the candidate as a full member of the Carthusian Order.

During his five years as postulant, novice and junior professed monk the candidate will have been studying,

---

[1] Simple vows are temporary, i.e. binding only for the period undertaken. The Carthusian vows are of obedience (which includes chastity and poverty) stability (i.e. loyalty to one's community) and conversion of manners (the turning of one's whole being to God).

[2] Until 1839 a one-year Novitiate before taking final vows was the rule, but this period was extended in 1851, 1924 and 1945, and to its present length in 1969. Records kept since the sixteenth century show that perseverance of professed monks has been of the order of 95 per cent, except for a small dip in the nineteenth century, down to 90 per cent.

[75]

among other things, for the priesthood if he was not already a priest. Assuming his acceptance into the Order at the final vote, he will need a further two years' study before he can be ordained. It will have taken him about nine and a half years to be able to celebrate his first Mass as a Carthusian Father, but the ultimate joys of such patience are sweet indeed.

Should someone who has taken vows in another religious order wish to test the Carthusian vocation, the rules are somewhat different. (The Carthusian Statues lay down: 'The religious who are or who have been in vows to another Order are not to be admitted to the Novitiate without the permission of the Reverend Father.'[1]) First he becomes a Postulant for three to five months and, if considered suitable, will undergo a five-year Novitiate. This is a longer Novitiate than that undertaken by a layman, since the Carthusians wish to ensure that anyone from another religious order does not bring into a Charterhouse too many rigid ideas acquired in his former order. After his fourth year in the Novitiate a vote will be taken, and if the community accepts him he will live with the solemn professed monks for a year, after which a final vote will be taken – in other words about five and a half years after his being accepted as a Postulant.

In general, all other religious orders will usually allow their members to climb a little higher up the ladder, so to speak, and leave to join the Carthusians. Carthusians, on the other hand, are most strongly discouraged from leaving their Charterhouses to join other orders.

A secular priest's period of apprenticeship is normally the same as for a layman entering the Order.

A would-be Converse Brother or Donate Brother wishing to enter the Order will undergo a six-month period of postulancy, at the end of which he must decide whether to

---

[1] The title by which the Minister-General of the Order is known.

opt for a Converse Brother's vocation, with the same binding vows as those of the Fathers, or to become a Donate. If he chooses the former, he spends two years as a Novice followed by three years with simple vows, renewed for a further two years if he is acceptable to the community. If after this seven-and-a-half year period of trial the community will still accept him, he makes solemn profession of vows for life.

After six months as a Postulant a Donate spends two years in the Novitiate, then makes three years' temporary donation followed by another two years' donation. At the end of this time he has an option: he can make a donation for life or decide to renew his donation every three years for the rest of his life.

It must be stressed that it is not uncommon for a man to become a Carthusian novice with the aim of becoming an ordained Father, but to decide, during the course of novitiate, that the vocation of a Brother was preferable.

Suitability of a candidate for the Carthusian Order is determined not only by the spirituality of the individual but also by his physical strength and mental stability. No one under the age of twenty is accepted, and no one over the age of forty-five, without special permission of the Superior of the Order. Today there is an increasing tendency in Charterhouses to insist that every novice be examined by a psychiatrist to ensure, if possible, that there is no religious quirk or obsession hidden in his subconscious which might emerge at a later date. The Carthusian Statutes declare:

> It is indeed certain that the progress or deterioration of the Order in the quality and in the number of its members chiefly depends on the good or bad reception and formation of Novices. . . . Among the qualities with which candidates for a life of solitude should be particularly endowed, sound and balanced judgement is particularly important.

[77]

# XII

## LA GRANDE CHARTREUSE

Mountain-built with peaceful citadel.

*Keats, 1795–1821*

I shall never forget my first visit to La Grande Chartreuse. I had already imbibed much of its history, partly from reading and partly from what I had learned from the monks of other Charterhouses. I had expected much, but my pilgrimage proved a greater and more wonderful experience than I could ever have imagined.

On the day of my arrival it was high summer and the sun shone brightly in a sky which was dazzlingly blue in the purity of the mountain air – pure, it seemed, as the air of paradise. As I drove from the hamlet of St Laurent du Pont the six miles to the monastery, up the foothills of the Dauphiné Alps through and across narrow gorges, I thought of centuries before, when Carthusian priors from all over Europe astride their horses, stumbling on the rocky track, had faced the dangers of marauding bears and wolves every two years to reach the mountainous height of La Grande Chartreuse to attend the General Chapters of the Order. Even more did I wonder at the fervour which must have inspired St Bruno to carve a virgin track through such terrain to this isolated yet devastatingly beautiful spot some nine hundred years earlier.

Coming upon La Grande Chartreuse itself, my first impressions were of how much bigger and more awe-inspiring it was, and how much more beautiful were its surroundings, compared with any of the photographs I had seen. I felt enveloped by the mantle of its tremendous

[78]

history. Yet, as I approached the great locked gate which was the entrance to the monastery, it was silence which reigned supreme; a silence of the world of the spirit and of an unparalleled richness.

Initial impressions apart, some of the memories I cherish the most include the privilege of seeing all over the monastery itself – something which, I was told, had been denied to a cardinal just before my arrival – but this was overshadowed by the favour of being invited to take my place in the choir stall for conventual Mass alongside the monks. To this day the solemn yet angelic singing of their plainchant re-echoes in my heart. I also recall the tenderness with which I was cared for in the guest house, and the glory of the sun rising in the east to shine upon the face of the Roche de l'Alien which towers above La Grande Chartreuse.

My most abiding memory, however, is of a steep climb up a rough path and over rocks to the little chapel which marks the site of St Bruno's original foundation, some two kilometres up the mountain from the monastery. Hot and thirsty from the climb, I drank water from a gentle natural spring close to the chapel where St Bruno and his companions must have drunk. With a key given to me by the monks I was able to enter the chapel and pray alone for a while at the ancient altar stone where St Bruno himself is believed to have prayed. As the ascent to the chapel can be tiring in summer, and is impassable in winter because of snow, few people visit it, but from time to time some of the monks make the trek to say their private Masses away from the world.

During its long history, La Grande Chartreuse has had more than its share of trials and tribulations: it has borne witness to fire, tempest, pestilence, pillaging and violent death. It seems almost as if God had specially selected the Carthusians to undergo such tests in order to show the world how the spirit can conquer all things.

Not quite fifty years after Bruno had established his first little foundation, it was destroyed by an avalanche in 1132. Many of the monks were killed, and the terrain was so difficult that it was twelve days before the survivors could be rescued. Relics of the dead are preserved in La Grande Chartreuse. The next monastery was the victim of fire in 1391, when many valuable books were destroyed. A further fire followed in 1473, and in 1562 the Carthusian mother house was pillaged by soldiers and set fire to once more. Yet a fourth fire occurred in 1592, but following a fifth fire in 1696 a solid stone monastery was built on the present site and opened in 1717. It is almost a small town in itself, enclosed within high walls; because it was erected at a time when there were some two hundred Charter-houses in Europe, the accommodation had to cater for all the Priors who came with their attendants and horses to participate in the General Chapters. The monastery itself covers 22 acres, while the land attached to it totals about 1,000 acres.

As with most communities, religious or secular, the Black Death took its toll of the monks,[1] and the building of the solid eighteenth-century monastery was by no means the end of Carthusian tribulations. After the French Revolution the monks of La Grande Chartreuse suffered expulsion in 1792, and along with monks from other Charterhouses many were executed and the remainder dispersed. When they were able to return, in 1816, they came back as 'tenants', and technically the Carthusians are still tenants to this day as La Grande Chartreuse is now a national monument belonging to the French state which contributes towards its upkeep.

Expelled once more in 1903 by Clemenceau's anti-clerical government, along with other religious orders, the monks of La Grande Chartreuse took refuge in Italy and it

---

[1] Some 900 Carthusians died in the Order as a whole.

was from the Italian Charterhouse of Farneta that Dom Michel Baglin, the Superior of the Carthusians, administered the Order. In 1901, the eight hundredth anniversary of the death of St Bruno, in anticipation of expulsion Dom Baglin wrote to the Prioress of the Carthusian nuns at Beauregard:

We are in the hands of God and protected by him we await the events which we fear. I believe that the tempest approaches – one which will be as terrible as a hurricane and one which will overturn many things. It will be the end of a certain number of institutions and also probably the end of a certain number of congregations. What will happen to us? Will we survive? Yes, of that I am certain. Perhaps we shall suffer but we shall escape destruction. The important thing is to pray and to pray a great deal. Our fate is in our own hands.

Strangely enough it was World War II which brought about the monks' return to La Grande Chartreuse. In the interim it had been something of an embarrassment to the French government, which had tried in turn to use the monastery as a holiday home and as a rest home for 'tired intellectuals' and in the 1930s had even attempted to sell it to the League of Nations! But in 1940 French people living in Italy, including monks, were advised to leave in view of Mussolini's impending entry into the war. The Minister-General of the Order, Dom Ferdinand Vidal, who was in Italy at the time, obtained permission from the French government to reoccupy La Grande Chartreuse and, requisitioned for the Carthusians by the local mayor, the monastery was entered once again on 10 June 1940, only for the whole area to be occupied by the German army three days later.

On the whole the Germans behaved well towards La Grande Chartreuse community although obtaining enough food was very difficult, particularly as the monks were feeding as well as sheltering members of the French Underground movement. The problem was partly solved, ironically enough, by the arrival at the monastery of personal friends of Hitler who came as sightseers with a 'letter of introduction' signed by the Führer himself. The Procurator entertained them to lunch – with Maquis partisans hiding in the cells below! Such was the respect in which the Procurator was subsequently held by the local Germans that he was able to travel freely in the area in search of food, assisted by Prioress Marie-Alphonse and the Carthusian nuns of neighbouring Beauregard. Now in his late seventies and at another French Charterhouse, where I had the honour of meeting him, the father concerned is still a great bulwark of the Order.

The war over, the Grande Chartreuse monks underwent a trial of a totally different nature when the monastery became a major tourist attraction. The silence of their beloved desert was rudely shattered, except during winter when the monastery was largely snowbound. But each spring and summer thousands of sightseers arrived from all over the world to ring the bell at the gate in the hope of visiting the famous monastery. They were drawn to it both by its great history and by the magnificent setting – cradled between mountains rising almost sheer on three sides, with the fourth side gazing down on the intervening valley.

The tourist problem was cleverly solved by turning the Courrerie into a museum; built on the site of an older hostelry of St Bruno's for his Lay Brothers, in the 1940s it was being used as a residence for aged and infirm Carthusians. Since the building was situated just over a mile below the monastery, the steep road up to La Grande Chartreuse was closed to motor traffic in general. The museum, open from May to October, is staffed by outsiders and attracts over 100,000 visitors each year. It acts as a kind of safety valve against the curious, thus preserving for the monks

'*La silence du désert des Pères Chartreux*', one of the corner-stones of their existence.

For those fortunate enough to obtain permission to visit La Grande Chartreuse – and I warn readers that this is very rarely given indeed, except to those who might feel they have a call to join the Order – some of the most inspiring and interesting parts of the monastery are the church itself, the great chapter-house and the library[1] where, although it is not as rich in treasures as that of Parkminster, I was able to see a twelfth-century breviary and thirteenth-century missals and admire the magnificent stained glass depicting the wide range of butterflies which abound in the area. Also of considerable interest is the Chapel of St Louis, presented to the Carthusians by King Louis XIII.

On the day I left that first time it happened that one of the monks passed away. On being told of his death I said how sorry I was to learn the sad news. I was gently rebuked: 'We are happy for him because he has gone to join his Father.' I could not help but meditate on the undeniable fact that the vast majority of the human race fears death. In the apt words of the boxer Joe Louis: 'Everyone wants to go to heaven but nobody wants to die.' Yet in La Grande Chartreuse and throughout the Charterhouses it has spawned, all Carthusians look forward with joy to death and to the day when they will no longer be halfway to heaven but in heaven itself for all eternity.

[1] Despite avalanches, fires, expulsions and other tribulations, the Carthusian Order is one of the best documented of all religious orders. Most of its archives are hidden from the public, but some of its oldest ones are to be found in the museums of Europe.

# XIII

## OFFSPRING OF LA GRANDE CHARTREUSE

May your house still keep a garrison of smiling children.

*Robert Louis Stevenson, 1850–94*

Since 1084, when St Bruno first hoisted the Carthusian standard at Chartreuse, there have been a total of 271 Carthusian foundations, including twenty-two houses for nuns, of which no fewer than 219 were established between 1100 and 1500. The maximum number of functioning monasteries at any one time was in the year 1514, when there were 196 Charterhouses, and when the number of monks and nuns in the Order must have amounted to some three thousand or more. Suppressions at different times totalled 210, principally during the French Revolution (eighty-two), the Reformation (forty-four) and under Napoleon (thirty-two), and in 1810 the order reached its lowest ebb when only eight houses remained occupied.[1]

Today there are twenty-three Charterhouses, including six housing Carthusian nuns. Since the last war, four new houses have been established, one each for monks in Germany and in the United States, and one each for nuns in France and Spain. A further new house for nuns in Italy is at present under consideration.

[1] There is some duplication in these figures as a number of Charterhouses were suppressed, reacquired and suppressed again. As the populations of Europe grew and new towns developed other Charterhouses were closed because solitude and silence had been destroyed. A number of these – particularly in Italy – are classified as national monuments.

All the various Charterhouses at which I have stayed and visited have radiated the same spirit of joyous holiness and brotherly (or sisterly) love. Yet each one holds its own special place in my memory. One Charterhouse with which I fell in love at first sight was that of Notre-Dame de Portes, the very first French daughter house of St Bruno's foundation. It was established in 1115 by two Benedictines, Bernard de Varey and Ponce from the Abbey D'Ambonay, in an area used by hermits between the fourth and eighth centuries and over 3,000 feet up in the Jura mountains, halfway between Lyons and Geneva. It is five miles from the nearest hamlet, nestling below the peak of the Molard de Don, from which Mont Blanc is visible at times. Both its architecture and the surrounding scenery reflect on the heart in a gentler way compared to the magnificence of La Grande Chartreuse. It was the first Charterhouse to be built in stone (in 1125), and although rebuilding was undertaken in 1646 it remains on its original site. The bones of a thousand or more monks lie in and around its cemetery.

The gentleness of the monks of Portes matched that of the monastery itself. Among many wonderful memories of my stay it is hard to select any which stand out more than the remainder, but there are, perhaps, two which come most readily to mind – both very different. The first is the imprint on both heart and mind, while in the choir stalls, of the rapture – almost ecstasy – on the faces of the monks opposite me as they sang during Mass. My second, perhaps surprisingly, is of the quite extraordinary profusion of butterflies of all kinds in the fields and woods surrounding the monastery. Their delicate beauty made me think that the garden of Eden could not have been so very different.

As with those in other Charterhouses, the Carthusians of Portes suffered many persecutions and, like others, the monastery was vandalised during the French Revolution

[85]

when the monks were dispersed. One heroic Carthusian, Dom Vallet, nevertheless heroically concealed himself in the monastery, aided by people from the villages below, for ten years until his death.

Following Clemenceau's expulsion of religious orders from France, Notre-Dame de Portes remained unoccupied by Carthusians for nearly fifty years. It was used as a hostel, a distillery, a farmhouse, and in the last war as a headquarters of the Maquis who actually executed collaborators in the monks' cells. It was eventually reacquired by the Order in 1951 in a state of considerable disrepair, and one of the monks from La Grande Chartreuse was sent there to act as 'janitor', so to speak, until a new community could be established. He remained there quite alone for fifteen years until repair work was put in hand. Finally, a new community was established in 1971, mainly with monks from the Charterhouse of Selignac. Today, as in the case of most Charterhouses, there is an international atmosphere with Swiss and English monks there alongside the French. A former doctor prays beside a former shepherd.

Notre-Dame de Portes owns a sizeable amount of forest land and the sale of timber is the monastery's main source of revenue. Forestry is one of the principal occupations of the Brothers, but once a month the Fathers are allowed to break their contemplative vigil and help them in their work.

Timber is also an important source of income for the new German Charterhouse of Marienau in Württemberg and of the Carthusians of the new Transfiguration monastery in Vermont, USA – the first Charterhouse in the New World. The former I have yet to visit; it was built to replace the Carthusian house near Düsseldorf which could no longer be used after an airport was built very close to it.

The Jugoslavian Charterhouse – Kartuzi Pleterje – is

the only one in a Communist country. That it is allowed to remain in Jugoslavia at all is solely the result of the shelter that the Prior at that time gave to Tito and his partisans during World War II. The monks help to provide for themselves by the sale of agricultural produce. In addition to Jugoslavs, the community includes Austrian, Dutch, French, German, Italian, Spanish and Swiss monks: a veritable United Nations house of prayer.

For most of its history the Carthusian Order, although always international, has attracted more French men and women to its ranks than people of other nationalities, but today there are more Spaniards than nationals of any other country. However, I do not wish to stress this point, for all Carthusians are first and foremost citizens of heaven.

Of the six Spanish Charterhouses – five for monks and one for nuns – I draw special attention to three: that of Miraflores in Burgos which, architecturally speaking, is probably the most resplendent of all Charterhouses – perhaps a little too much so when considering the simplicity of the Carthusian lifestyle. Yet Miraflores is virtually self-supporting, and one of its sources of revenue is the sale of rosaries made of beads fashioned from dried and crushed rose petals. It has, of course, suffered persecution like all Charterhouses, but probably rather less than other Spanish houses. It was one of sixteen houses suppressed in 1835–6, during the Spanish and Portuguese revolutions, but several of the monks succeeded in remaining in Miraflores by adopting the black habits of the ordinary parish priests.

In contrast to Miraflores, the Cartuja de Montelegro in the Barcelona area is one of the poorest centres of Carthusian life. Except for vegetables it is not self-supporting in any way, and exists on donations from La Grande Chartreuse. One of the oldest Charterhouses, it was established in 1415 and the hostelry attached to it is based on a former castle belonging at one time to Charlemagne. In the course of Miraflores' more than 550 years' history, the monks have been subject to expulsion at various times – particularly during the nineteenth century. In 1909 it was set fire to, and during the Spanish Civil War six of its monks were taken out and shot by the Communists.

One special Spanish treat still in store for me is a visit to the nuns at the Cartuja de Benifaça in Tarragona. Completely isolated in an area of great beauty, Benifaca was originally a Cistercian abbey founded in 1233. Suppressed in 1835, it was acquired by the Carthusians in 1967, despite being in a very dilapidated state, on account of its isolation and freedom from tourist traffic. The reconstruction of Benifaca undertaken by the Carthusians has enabled the nuns to have the same type of solitary hermitages as do the monks of the Order. From correspondence I have had with Benifaca, and from photographs I have been privileged to receive from there, it is abundantly clear that the good nuns of this Charterhouse are as joyfully holy as their Sisters whom I have met in the communities for Carthusian nuns in Italy.

My first encounter with the Carthusian nuns was at the Certosa di San Francesco, which lies 1,000 feet up on a lonely Piedmontese hill. A former Capuchin monastery, built on the site of a much older one dating from the twelfth century which, according to tradition, was founded by St Francis of Assisi himself, it was acquired by the Carthusians in 1903. Though originally intended as a house of refuge for the nuns of Beauregard, an entirely new community of nuns was established there in 1912, which has thrived in peace ever since except for an incursion by German soldiers following Italy's collapse in the last war. The Germans were concerned that the nuns were sheltering Italian partisans – which was not the case, as it happens – and sent a hail of rifle bullets through the windows of the convent itself. By great fortune none of the nuns was killed or wounded.

On my arrival at San Francesco I felt a welcoming warmth radiating from this beautiful and relatively small monastery with its cream-painted walls and pink-tiled roof. Winter there is cold, but in summer flowers abound and a magnificent magnolia tree stands in front of the entrance to the chapel attached to the monastery. By order of the Bishop of Turin the chapel is open to the public, but in this isolated spot – difficult to find even with a map – few outsiders visit it.

Although the nuns' choir remains hidden from view and behind a grille, a visit to the San Francesco chapel for Mass or Vespers provides a rare opportunity for the ordinary public to hear the ancient Carthusian Gregorian chant. I have listened to the beautiful and renowned singing of Benedictine nuns of the Solesmes congregation, but here on this isolated Italian hill there was something indefinably transcendental about the spirituality of the singing which I have not heard from any nuns but Carthusians.

As in every Charterhouse, I was tenderly cared for in the little guest house at San Francesco and provided with lovingly prepared food. I also had the privilege of talking with some of the nuns, marvelling at their joyful serenity and good humour; the beauty of their countenances reflected the love in their hearts. I was only sorry that time did not permit me to visit Vedana, a former Charterhouse for monks in the Venice area to which some of the San Francesco community were detached a few years ago to live in individual hermitages as an experiment, a replica of the life of the Fathers of the Order. From all the accounts I received, the experiment was proving most successful.

If anything – and the difference was marginal! – my reception by the nuns at the Certosa di Riva was even more welcoming than at San Franceso. Though equally isolated, the Riva Charterhouse differs from San Fran-

[89]

cesco in two respects: unlike most houses[1] it is situated on
flat ground in a plain, and the nuns there have a number of
solitary hermitages built in 1977 on the lines of those for
the Order's Fathers – a provision which they greatly welcome.

At Riva, I had the great privilege – and one only
accorded to the Carthusian vicar attached to the monastery once a year on the occasion of the Bishop of Turin's
annual visit – of being allowed inside the nuns' enclosure.[2]
The peace and beauty of the garden with its small pond,
and of the hermitage which I was shown, was almost
overwhelming. Even the adjacent orchard and vegetable
garden were creations of unusual beauty. These only yield
enough produce for the nuns' own consumption, but a
certain amount of hay is sold to local farmers in exchange
for milk with which the nuns make their own butter and
cheese.

On the occasion of my visit, the Riva community was
awaiting the arrival of a novice from the United States. I
began to understand the power of the Holy Spirit which
was drawing a young woman thousands of miles to abandon this world to live in silent contemplation of God for
the rest of her days.

Sadly, because of the development nearby of a motorway, the historic Beauregard Charterhouse for nuns had to
be closed in 1973. A new haven to replace it has been built
at Reillane in the Alps of Haute-Provence.

In England there is today only one Charterhouse, that
of St Hugh's, Parkminster, in Sussex. A comparatively

---

[1] St Bruno recommended communities to select sites that were high up
partly because of their isolation and partly because such sites would give a
greater sense of nearness to heaven.
[2] A concession that the Prioress obtained for me from her bishop. Even
during his bi-annual visitation, the visitor (a Carthusian Prior) may not
enter a nuns' enclosure and only talks with members of the community in
the parlour.

new foundation – the church was consecrated in 1883 – it was, and still is, the first Charterhouse to be established in England since the Carthusians were martyred or expelled and their monasteries laid waste in the days of Henry VIII.

The planning of the new English Charterhouse began in 1869 when the Carthusians in France feared – quite rightly as it turned out – that a renewed persecution of religious orders was in the offing. Parkminster, whose foundation stone was laid in 1877, was intended as a house of refuge for the Carthusians of France should religious orders be expelled. For this reason St Hugh's is the largest of all the Charterhouses, and must be one of the largest monasteries in the world. One of its most striking features is the great cloister – to give some idea of its size, it encloses a $3\frac{1}{2}$-acre orchard. With its towering 200-foot spire, the Parkminster church is perhaps the most stately in the order, not excepting that of La Grande Chartreuse itself. As for its library of some thirty thousand religious books,[1] this must be the finest single library belonging to any religious order in the world. I have had the closest of relations over the years with the monks of Parkminster, and much of this book has been researched within its walls. St Hugh's will always remain my second home.

To give a complete account of the history and special attributes of every Charterhouse would require a book to itself, but I hope that in this and in Chapter XII I have revealed enough about a cross-section of Charterhouses to give the reader a clear picture of the units and the souls within them that make up this most holy yet most self-effacing of all religious orders.

There is one more Charterhouse, however, of which I must tell – the new Charterhouse of the Transfiguration in

---

[1] Many of the books at Parkminster originate from the library of King Victor-Emanuel I of Italy, whose collection was purchased by the first Prior of Parkminster in a privately negotiated sale.

Vermont. If this is given a chapter of its own it is because the United States is one of the two most powerful nations in the world, and also a land of many and often conflicting religions. The arrival in America of the purest form of contemplative life, and its spreading, could, one hopes, prove of great benefit to the American people and, in consequence, to the whole world.

# XIV

# A CHARTERHOUSE IN THE NEW WORLD

Leaving the old, both worlds at once they view
That stand upon the threshold of the new.

*Edmund Walker, 1606–87*

The saga of how the Carthusians came to establish themselves in the New World is a fascinating one indeed. In
1950 La Grande Chartreuse received a letter from a
woman in the United States offering property for the
foundation of an American Charterhouse. As a result
Father Thomas Moore, an American Carthusian belonging to the Miraflores community, was sent across the
Atlantic to investigate. At his first meeting with the
woman Father Moore, who had formerly been a well-
known psychiatrist, quickly realised that she was mentally
unbalanced and had neither property nor money to offer.
But divine providence was at hand: hearing of Father
Moore's presence in Vermont, another woman gladly gave
the Carthusians 500 acres and a farmhouse set in a wild
part of the state. Here Father Moore, joined by another
Father and two Brothers from Europe, nourished the
infant Carthusian foundation.

Even for a Carthusian, Father Moore was an exceptional man. Trained as a doctor, during World War I he
served in the US Army Medical Corps where he
specialised in psychiatry. He joined the Benedictines in
1922 at the age of forty-five. The author of many books on
psychiatry, he founded a number of rehabilitation centres

[93]

for the mentally ill and also a school for retarded girls. In 1947 he was lecturing in Madrid, and decided to spend a brief retreat at Miraflores. The mantle of Bruno fell on his shoulders and in 1949 – despite the fact that he was seventy-two – because of his unusual talents and spirituality he was allowed to join the ranks of fully professed Carthusians. He was to write: 'I made more progress in the interior life in one year at Miraflores than in all the rest of my life.'

Father Moore spent ten years getting the Carthusians off the ground in the United States. He returned to Miraflores in 1960, when the American monastery had been opened below the summit of Mount Equinox. Then an old man of eighty-three, he continued to attend the night office every night of his life until he was ninety; he died in 1969, aged ninety-one. At Miraflores, they said of him, '*El ha muerta con la muerto de los santos.*' (He died the death of the saints.)

In the early days of the American Carthusian community, while the Brothers lived in the farmhouse the Fathers lived in little shanties they had built in the woods round about, reminiscent of Bruno's original band of Carthusians. The monastery was set in one of the coldest parts of America, with up to 30°C of frost in the winter, and one of the American Carthusians told me what an inspiring sight it was to see the elderly Father Moore battling his way through a snowstorm to church for the night office, and then at 2 a.m. battling his way back again to his little shanty.

After the original donation to the Carthusians of 500 acres, a few years later the order gladly accepted an American shipping magnate's gift of a further adjacent 800 acres. Some purchases of land increased the acreage to 2,000, and plans for the building of a monastery were put in hand. Divine providence, however, was to intervene once again in the form of a gift of 6,500 acres, also in Vermont, surrounding Mount Equinox, from which on a clear day one can see thirty miles in all directions without another building in sight. The owner, a childless millionaire from one of America's leading chemical combines, was fearful that the beautiful forest land he had acquired on his retirement would be spoilt by commercial developers after his death. He felt that in the hands of the Carthusians, whose way of life had not changed through the centuries, his beloved nature reserve which abounded in wildlife would remain equally unchanged through the centuries to come. With funds provided by La Grande Chartreuse, and with a nucleus of monks from Europe, soon to be joined by new entrants to the order from within America itself, the new foundation took shape.

In some ways I found it an even greater privilege to stay at the Charterhouse of the Transfiguration than at the other Charterhouses which I have been fortunate enough to visit. In America, any visits except from those thinking of joining the order are very rare indeed. I had expected to find some difference between an American Charterhouse and those in Europe; there was – but not quite of the kind I had anticipated. Carthusian life and spirituality were indeed the same as in all Charterhouses, but I soon sensed an even greater determination to maintain the Carthusian desert than I had observed elsewhere; a determination that under no circumstances would the materialistic American way of life encroach upon the monks' seclusion.

Unimpeded by European traditions, the simplistic architecture of the monastery, both within and without, is something of an eye-opener in its starkness and imbues a great sense of what the Carthusians call rusticity. Adhering to elementary Carthusian principles, the Charterhouse of the Transfiguration creates an aura of the hermitic caves of the desert, and I sensed that St Bruno was looking down on it with approval. As I took my place in the choir stalls for Mass I could feel the spirits of the Desert Fathers in attendance, and it was with no surprise when I learned later that the local Bishop of Burlington ascribed all the good in his diocese to the presence in it of the Carthusians.

As in most Charterhouses, the community of the Transfiguration has a distinctly international flavour. Although predominantly American, the Vermont Carthusians include a Frenchman, a German, a Norwegian and a New Zealander. Similarly, the monks come from many walks of life: soldier, artist, hunter, farmer, cinema owner, singer, Jew from Brooklyn. (Several are former Trappists, who became somewhat disillusioned with the watering down of Cistercian life in America following Thomas Merton's popularity, which led to less austerity and more openness in that order.)

As regards work, apart from tending to the needs of the monastery itself, the Brothers concentrate on the vast acreage of forestry, while the Fathers, who have little time for physical work other than chopping wood for the fires in their cells, do a certain amount of bookbinding.

The great paradox which overhangs Carthusian life in the United States is that, whereas more and more Americans are opening their hearts to the contemplative ideal, only the tiniest handful of the population can be aware of the Carthusian presence in its midst. Expansion through pollination from the flower of St Bruno, so firmly planted in Vermont, may prove difficult without some degree of publicity and without opening the doors of the monastery every now and then to bishops and to specially approved priests to undertake periodic retreats, so that afterwards they may spread the news about the Carthusian way.

Only a little thought is required to realise the dangers that could arise from such publicity in a country like America, were the Carthusian presence too widely known. Not only could it arouse the curiosity of tourists but it might also encourage many ersatz Postulants who were either just idly curious or had a superficial emotional attraction which would quickly evaporate.

I discussed this problem at some length with the Prior, and it is right that he should have the last word on the subject. Here, verbatim, are his comments:

> There is a certain quality about Carthusian reclusion which is even greater than that of ordinary solitude and which seems to be lost when you open the door. Our silence can profit the world without speaking. There is a certain grace about the Carthusian vocation and it seems to me that fidelity to that grace brings more to the world and more to those seeking retreats than a slight watering down of our ideal for the sake of helping retreatants directly.

# XV

# THE CARTHUSIAN ORDER: ORGANISATION AND MANAGEMENT

See how our works endure.

*Rudyard Kipling, 1865–1936*

Although I believe I have now given the reader a good idea of the way in which Carthusians spend their days, there remain a number of unanswered questions. What keeps the wheels of the monastery turning? Who pays for building repairs and electricity bills? Where does the monks' food and clothing come from? What happens when they get toothache or need spectacles? Do they read newspapers? Do they ever see their families? What are the relationships between a Charterhouse and the Pope, La Grande Chartreuse, or the local bishop?

At the level of the individual Charterhouse, each is presided over by a Prior elected by the monks themselves – both Fathers and Brothers. Like the captain of a ship, he has overall responsibility for the monastery and for the spiritual and other needs of all the monks entrusted to his care. The Carthusian Order has always resisted suggestions from Rome and elsewhere that their Priors should be elevated to abbots – who rank with bishops – in view of the pomp and ceremonial that this might entail at times. To quote the Carthusian Statutes: 'By his own docility to the spirit, he [the Prior] should mirror to all the love of Christ.'

[98]

To assist him, the Prior appoints some of his monks to various posts of responsibility within the monastery. First is his deputy, the Vicar, who is normally a senior Father and may well be a former Prior. 'The Vicar', it is laid down in the Statutes, 'shall be in word and deed a shining example to the rest, maintaining all in regular observance and holy peace.' Also to help the Prior in the administration of his Charterhouse there is a Prior's Council – essentially a small committee consisting of the Prior himself, the Vicar, the Procurator, one Father or Brother chosen by the Prior and one Father or Brother elected by the community as a whole.

The most occupied man in a Charterhouse is probably the Procurator. He is the monk to whom the Prior delegates the task of attending to all material matters relating to the monastery, and he is the main link with the outside world.

Under the Prior's direction the Procurator supervises the work of the Brothers. He must deal with the maintenance of the building, pay all bills and keep the monastery's accounts. And, although delegating much to the two Brothers who work in the kitchen, he has overall control of what the monks eat and must ensure that no luxuries are brought into the monastery even if they come as gifts.

To reduce the necessity of leaving the monastery walls to the bare minimum, the Procurator will do most of the ordering of supplies on the telephone. When a monk needs to visit a doctor, dentist or an optician, he will try to arrange for a layman to take him by car.

In short the Procurator, even if he has an assistant Procurator to help him, is a busy man and has to sacrifice much of the solitude and silence he desires so that the other monks in his Charterhouse can enjoy theirs. His attitude is best summed up by the Benedictine Abbot Chapman, who once said, 'I wish I could join the "solitaries" [on Caldy Island], instead of being Superior and having to write books. But I don't wish to have what I wish, of course.'

Other important offices in a Charterhouse include that of Novice Master, who bears the heavy responsibility of caring for the spiritual guidance and testing of Novices. The Sacristan tends to the monastery church and tolls the bell for the various offices, while two Cantors lead the chant in choir. Yet another monk will be in charge of a normally large library of spiritual books.

Charterhouses throughout the world are free of any allegiances to cardinals, archbishops or bishops in the countries in which they are situated; their Priors are directly responsible to the Superior of the Order, the Prior of La Grande Chartreuse who is known as the Reverend Father. A Procurator-General for the whole Order is appointed to liaise with the Pope and the Vatican authorities, and lives in the vicinity of Rome.

In all countries where there are religious orders, there is a Council of the Superiors – in effect a committee – which meets from time to time to consider the attitudes to be adopted towards important aspects of life, religious and lay, in their respective countries. Carthusian Priors are, *ipso facto*, members of these councils but, true to their Statutes' command, never leave their monasteries except for the most important of reasons – rarely, if ever, attend any council meetings.

Turning to the financial front, many Charterhouses have been endowed by benefactors. Such endowments, together with support from the monks' own works, means that some are self-sufficient or largely so, while others are mainly supported by central funds from La Grande Chartreuse, receiving quarterly grants known as dotations.

It is a complete fallacy that the Carthusian Order is financed mainly from the sale of green and yellow Chartreuse liqueurs. Until the French Revolution Charterhouses had been supported by wealthy benefactors and by the monks' own work in agriculture, forestry and even mining enterprises. After the Revolution, the Order was extremely poor – so poor, in fact, that Novices had to buy their own habits. It was only in the nineteenth century that the French army[1] 'discovered' the pleasures of drinking the age-old Chartreuse liqueurs which the monks used to distil for themselves from an ancient recipe – 'top secret', in newspaper jargon – dating back to at least 1605 and involving some one hundred and thirty different herbs. The liqueurs are produced both at Voiron, near La Grande Chartreuse and, after the expulsion of religious orders from France at the beginning of this century, also at Tarragona in Spain, supervised in each case by three Carthusian brothers. The recipe is still a zealously guarded secret.[2]

Although revenue arising from Chartreuse liqueurs was a good source of income to the Carthusians in the last century, today liqueurs have become increasingly unfashionable and increasingly expensive; their manufacture only produces some fifteen per cent of the Order's revenue. Needless to say the monks are not in any way involved in the sale of liqueurs which is entirely in the hands of a commercial undertaking.

Every two years, a council called a General Chapter is held at La Grande Chartreuse which is attended by all the priors of the Order and, nowadays, generally some representatives of the Brothers. The General Chapter usually lasts about two weeks and reviews the progress of the Order in all its facets with a view to strengthening any possible weaknesses, both spiritual and material, which might be tending to develop. Immediately following the monks' General Chapter the Prioresses of the monasteries

---

[1] Chartreuse was also found to be an excellent cure for army horses with colic, and was much used for this purpose during the Crimean War.
[2] On the occasion of the expulsion of 1901 the monks of La Grande Chartreuse cleverly polluted the vaults, so that the state could not take over the manufacture of the liqueurs.

for nuns meet for their own General Chapter, presided over by the Superior of the Order in a guest house outside the walls of La Grande Chartreuse.

To ensure that Carthusian monasteries fully live up to the spiritual demands and obediences of the Order, a visitor, together with a deputy, both from other Carthusian monasteries and normally both Priors, make a Visitation to each monastery every two years to make an independent check on the life and discipline of the community as a whole and of each individual monk. This system of Visitations was established, together with the bi-annual General Chapter, as long ago as 1176, and the extreme care with which novices are accepted has ensured the Order's unique spiritual purity through the centuries. Even the Superior of the Order is not immune from admonishment or, indeed, removal from office, if it is considered that he is not living up to the highest possible Carthusian standards such as are demanded of his position.

It has been said many times that the Carthusian Order has never been reformed because it has never been deformed ('*Religio Cartusianorum nunquam reformata quia nunquam deformata*'). In fact it can be argued that the opposite is really the case: they have a policy of non-stop reform, in the sense that the slightest tendency towards deformation of any aspect of Carthusian life has always been stamped on at birth. The Papal Bulls of Alexander IV in 1257 and Pius II in 1460 eulogising the Carthusian Order were reaffirmed by Pius XI in 1924: 'Unlike other religious orders that Order has never in so long a space of time needed any amendment or, as they say, reform.'

Turning to the question of health, if a monk falls ill he is tended in his cell by his fellow monks, and by the infirmarian in particular, unless a really serious illness necessitates going to hospital. This rarely happens; the Carthusian life of austerity and prayer keeps the monks remarkably fit, and as a rule they live to a ripe old age.

The Carthusian Statutes are very specific about the care to be given a sick monk:

> Sickness and the infirmities of old age invite us to a new act to trust in confidence in our Heavenly Father who by means of these infirmities conforms us ever more perfectly to Christ. The Prior will show a special kindness towards the sick and the aged, and towards those who are being purified by some trial. In all matters, however personal, in which they cannot take care of themselves let them be humbly helped. Let them realise that just as healthy monks differ from healthy lay folk so too should sick monks differ from sick lay folk. The sick then are to be asked to bear in mind the sufferings of Christ, those who look after them the compassion of Christ.
>
> Let us commit ourselves in a docile spirit to the will of God, remembering that the trial of infirmity prepares us for the joys of eternity.

The Carthusians abstain totally from all meat, and once a week – normally on Fridays – live on dry bread and water. From 14 September until Easter they enjoin the great monastic fast: one meal per day plus a piece of dry bread with a drink of some kind in the evening. In Advent and Lent no dairy foods are permitted.

Pope Urban V once wished to amend the Carthusian rule of perpetual abstinence from meat, but the Carthusians, sensing that their ancient discipline might be weakened, sent a deputation on foot to the Pope to protest. The deputation consisted of twenty-seven monks whose ages ranged from eighty-eight to ninety-five. The Pope quickly abandoned his idea!

Carthusian austerity, in line with that of the Desert Fathers, aims to bring the soul in contact with the ultimate good of God and the imperfections of the body into contact with penance, which raises the body near to the region of the spirit. Mortification in the manner of the Puritans or the 'Wee Frees' of Scotland is little less than spiritual

[103]

pride. True mortification in the Carthusian manner is a 'non-attachment' to the flesh or, in the words of St Francis de Sales – 'holy indifference'. Christ himself said: 'There is no way of casting out bad spirits as this except by prayer and fasting.' Mortification of the flesh has been laid down in Christian, Buddhist and Hindu writings as an essential step to achieving a higher state. The taming of the body helps the soul to be fed.

Like other religious, in quitting the world for God the Carthusian takes leave of his family, although they are never forgotten in his prayers and there is a special guest house attached to his monastery where members of his family may come to stay for two days and nights[1] in any one year. I have myself seen how much joy and happiness these reunions bring to everyone concerned. But to the Carthusian, although family relationships are very important, his relationship with God is on a different and higher plane.

Although the Carthusians generally are forbidden to read newspapers and have no television or radio, the Statutes lay down that communities should be advised of news items of major importance. To meet this requirement, Priors alone will read some serious-minded newspaper or weekly magazine and, at their discretion, will circulate to the members of their communities details of events in the outside world.

In addition to prayer sung or said, and on occasions when a few words may need to be exchanged in the course of his duties, a Carthusian breaks silence a little more often than may be supposed. On Sundays, after their midday meal and a sermon or reading from the Statutes in chapter, the monks assemble together in a room set aside for the purpose for what is called recreation, when for an hour to

---

[1] Effectively three days if one takes into account the day of arrival and day of departure.

an hour and a half they will talk together about many things, exchanging reminiscences of the past week or of years gone by. And, of course, the Fathers talk together on Mondays, when they go for a three-hour walk (spatiamentum) outside the monastery. The Brothers, who take more physical exercise in the course of their routine obediences, take a similar walk once a month. Once a year the entire community goes for what is known as the long walk, when it sets off for a whole day. As the long walk may last six or seven hours and cover a number of miles, the monks take a picnic lunch with them.

On a more mundane front, the provision of such items as habits, shoes, soap, razor blades etc. lies within the procurator's province. Habits are usually made within the monastery from cloth purchased outside; socks and underwear are bought or may be gifts; shoes, sometimes specially made with an extra middle sole of cork, also come from outside. (The cork is to provide insulation against the often bitter winter cold, when the monks in some Charterhouses are at their night vigil in unheated churches.) The Fathers, but not the Brothers, wear hair shirts.[1]

Carthusians, unlike most religious today, are tonsured and have their heads shaved with an electric razor once a fortnight. This practice, known as rasura, leaves a stubble effect on the head; there is no resemblance to the Yul Brynners of this world!

All monks attend to the cleaning of their own cells and simple clothing repairs. As we have already seen, some Brothers are trained to handle tailoring or the cobbling of footwear.

The Fathers chop their own wood for their fires which will be partially supplemented with coal; Brothers usually

[1] Made from canvas interwoven with hair from horses' tails. The material is made outside the monastery and the hair shirts themselves are made up by the monks.

[105]

have paraffin stoves[1] in their cells. Cells only contain cold water taps, but hot water is available for fortnightly baths. These apart, should a monk wish to have some hot water to shave or to wash in the winter, he must heat it himself on his fire.

When he dies, the Carthusian is buried in his habit in a cemetery within the confines of his monastery. Be he Brother, Father, Prior or Superior of the whole Order, his habit in death, as in life, is the same. A simple cross without a name marks the spot. No one will ever know how many saints have been buried anonymously within the walls of Charterhouses. Their cemeteries remind us once again of that Carthusian motto: 'To make saints not to publicise them'.

Needless to say, Carthusian monks do not have holidays. As one monk once remarked: 'I have a perpetual holiday, living in the House of God.'

Despite the solitude and silence, life in a Carthusian monastery appears to be quite animated to those who live in one. The monks often complain they do not have enough time to get through all the things they wish to in a day.

The religious who is engaged in prayer and penance scarcely perceives the lapse of time as it passes rapidly on towards eternity. When at length he quits his cell for heaven he will not feel that the journey there has been long or tedious.

I can vouchsafe that despite their reclusion – or perhaps I should say because this carries them to such a high state of Godly love – I have never met such happy, joyful and good-humoured people anywhere. The sense of brotherly (or sisterly) love in all the Charterhouses I have visited much exceeds that of any other religious community with which I have been in contact – with no disrespect to the latter, I hasten to add!

[1] With up to seven hours a day manual work already, having to chop wood for their cells as well would cut into the Brothers' time for prayer.

# XVI

# CARTHUSIAN
# SPIRITUALITY: A SUMMARY

God himself is the unchangeable and eternal
contemplative; the Carthusian sits at his feet
like Mary at Bethany.

*A Carthusian*

As the only exclusively contemplative religious order in
the world today – is it a coincidence that it is the only one
that has never had to be reformed and is totally true to its
founder's original principles? – the Carthusian's contemplative role in life is, to quote St Gregory the Great
(540–607): 'To mingle with the heavenly citizens and to
rejoice at its everlasting incorruption in the sight of God'.

The world's coastline is dotted with lighthouses and the
lighthouse-keepers who tend them are essential in prevent-
ing ships from running on to reefs and into shallows.
Contemplative monks in Charterhouses likewise perform
an invaluable service in offering up to God their lives in
prayer, so that the rest of mankind may not break its back
on the reefs of godlessness. Both lighthouses and Charterhouses are vital in this world, but just as all men are not
meant to be lighthouse-keepers all are not called to be
Carthusians. At the same time, while we probably have
enough lighthouse-keepers, we could well do with more of
like mind to the Carthusians.

Those who do not understand the call to silence think of
it as emptiness, but it is this emptying out of earthly
vapidness which creates room for the reality of the spirit to

[107]

enter; then all is full in abundance. The whole purpose of the Carthusian Order is to help souls to detach themselves from this world into union with God. The enclosure, the habit, silence, fasting, abstinence, vigils, discipline, chastity, poverty and obedience lead to isolation and separation from all outward things, so that there is no room left for anything but God.

The Carthusian devotes many hours in prayer each day to make good the defect left by mankind in general, for he has been chosen by God to fulfil the role of recalling man to the basic purpose of his existence by his own more complete dedication to spiritual matters. Far from mankind, he lives in holy abandonment in order to be near to God, and yet near to God on behalf of those who are far from God.

God is the unlimited source of all that is good, and the Carthusians set up a kind of pipeline between this reservoir and keep it open by prayer and by total surrender to God. They give a guarantee to the heart of the Church of a permanent ministry of prayer, their function being described by the Council of Vatican II as 'a secret apostolic fecundity'. In the words of the Carthusian Statutes:

> By our total surrender, we profess before the world and witness to the ultimate reality of God. Our God-given joy in loving and serving him exclusively proves to the world that his gifts are a reality which can replace most of the so-called necessities of worldly life. It proves that the spiritual life is an everyday reality.

It is surprising how many people write to Charterhouses just to say how the mere knowledge of the existence of Carthusians and of the fact that they pray day and night deepens their faith. Many also write that requests for prayers directed to Charterhouses are answered. For this I can vouch personally. Some years ago, after a seemingly never-ending series of operations on my eyes, I feared I would go blind. The day I learned that my request to the Carthusians to pray for my sight had been accepted, I had no more fears and no more operations. Of the millions who must have only visited the Museum of La Grande Chartreuse, one cannot begin to guess at the numbers whose faith must have been restored or strengthened from learning just a little about these saintly men.

In trying to sum up the depth and core of Carthusian spirituality I can do no better than quote from the pages of the Statutes of the order and from Guiges' *Consuetudines*, with which the Statutes are so much imbued. Here are a few extracts:

> Solitude of some sort is essential to the seeker after God. There is no way that leads more certainly to contemplation. . . .
>
> As we contemplate all the benefits which God has prepared for those whom God has called into the desert, let us rejoice with Bruno our blessed father that we have attained the peaceful lake whose waters well up with the purest sources of the spirit, untroubled by news coming from outside, and like a clear mirror reflect one image only, that of Christ. . . .
>
> We know moreover that in our vocation of humility it does not become us to teach, but rather to be taught, and it is much better to celebrate the merits of our neighbours than our own. . . .
>
> The principal application of our vocation is to live in silence and solitude in ourselves and as in the words of Jeremiah: 'A solitary will sit down and keep silence'. . . .
>
> We must testify to the world, excessively absorbed in earthly things, that there is no God but Him. Our life shares something of the joys of Heaven. . . .
>
> Apart from all, to all we are united so that it is in the name of all that we stand before the haven of a hidden port, in which we are invited to experience in some sort the incomparable beauty of the supreme good. . . .
>
> The benefits, the divine delights that solitude and the

silence of the hermitage bring to those who love them, only those who have experienced them can tell, yet in choosing this the best part, it is not our advantage alone that we have in view. In embracing the hidden life, we do not abandon our great family of fellow men. On the contrary, by devoting ourselves exclusively to God we exercise a special function in the Church, where things seen are ordered to things unseen and exterior activity to contemplation. . . .

In solitude then let the monk's soul be like a tranquil living God. . . . Our life clearly shows that something of the joys of Heaven is present already here below. . . .

Wherefore in praise of God, for which the hermit Order of Carthusians was founded in a special way, let us dedicate ourselves to the peace and silence of our cells and strive to offer him unceasing worship so that sanctified in truth we may be those true worshippers which the Father seeks.

The final chapter of the *Consuetudines* is a eulogy of the solitary life, and Guiges cites many authorities as witnesses to this being the ideal state:

We know from the Old Testament and also from the New Testament that nearly all the higher secrets and the deepest revelations come to people not in the tumult of crowds but when they have found themselves alone. The servants of God when they wished to meditate more deeply on some truth or to pray more truly, or to escape from the things of this world in order to be ravished in the spirit, always avoided multitudes and sought the advantages of solitude.

Guiges refers to Isaac going alone to meditate in the fields, and to Jacob, who in solitude 'met God face to face and in one moment of solitude gained a greater blessing from God than in the whole of the rest of his life which passed among men.' References are also made to the love of solitude of Moses, Elijah and Elisha, and to the divine secrets revealed to them when they drew themselves apart from mankind. He quotes these glorious words of Jeremiah: 'It is good to wait in silence for the greeting of God. . . . He who sits alone and keeps silence will rise above himself.'

We are reminded by Guiges of John the Baptist's life in the wilderness and, of course, of Christ himself going up into the mountain to pray alone, and of how at the hour of the Passion he again left the Apostles in order to pray in solitude. The joys of the solitary life of the Desert Fathers are much extolled.

Guiges ends this great eulogy in the following words: 'There is nothing better one can choose in life than solitude with the soft sweetness of the Psalms, the application to reading, the fervour of prayer, the depth of meditation, the transport of contemplation, and the baptism of tears.' Here indeed is striking testimony to the primacy of contemplation and the riches of its spiritual wisdom.

It was the Benedictine Father Augustine Baker (1575–1641), the author of *Sancta Sophia* (Holy Wisdom), who wrote:

> Those that are inexperienced may and often do call contemplation a state of idleness and unprofitable cessation as Martha complained against her sister Mary, but those who have attained to a taste of it know it to be 'the business of all businesses' as St Bernard called it. Those inexpressible devotions which they exercise in which they tacitly involve the needs of the whole Church are far more prevailing with God than the busy endeavours and prayers of ten thousand others. A few such secret and unknown servants of God are the chariots and horsemen, the strength and bulwarks of the kingdom of churches where they live.

The comments on the Carthusians of the Oratorian, Père Charles de Condren (1588–1641) are also very pertinent:

> The dwelling amidst the mountains of La Grande Chartreuse is not an abode for the people of the world. It needs

[111]

a being who is all soul to live in such a spot. But when this paradise has been reached, there is nothing more to hope for on earth. You may come from where you will in the world, even from its holiest shrines, but once arrived at this House of God, the gate of Heaven, you must become a saint or you never will become one anywhere.

Popes without number have testified to the great Carthusian spirituality. Pope Celestine III told of the purity of their lives 'in the heights of contemplation', while it was probably Pope Innocent III who first referred to the Martha and Mary analogy when he wrote: 'You have left the duties of Martha engaged in many things choosing rather to remain with Mary at the feet of the Lord, listening to his words.' It was John XXII who spoke of 'the spotlessness of their innocent lives'. Yet another Pope, Innocent IV, eulogised the Carthusians when he wrote of them 'lighting up the Church with striking splendour, shining with purity of life, burning with the fervour of charity. . . . Dead to the world, they live for Christ. . . . In the height of their contemplation they sit at the feet of the Lord.'

More recently, the *Umbratilem* of Pope Pius XI, often called 'the Magna Carta for contemplatives', in approving the revised Carthusian Statutes of 1924, contained these words:

No more perfect state and rule of life than that can be proposed to men to take up and embrace if the Lord calls them to it. They who assiduously fulfil the duty of prayer and penance contribute much more to the increase of the Church and welfare of mankind than those who labour in tilling the master's field for, unless the former drew down from Heaven a shower of divine graces to water the field that is being tilled, the evangelical labourers would reap forsooth from their toil a mere scanty crop. . . . For, if ever it was needful that there should be anchorites of that sort in the Church of God, it is most specially nowadays when we see so many Christians living without a thought for the things of the next world and utterly regardless of their eternal salvation ... they silently fulfil that apostolate which is the most universal and the most fruitful of all in the Church.

Giving formal approval to the latest Carthusian Statutes (1971), Pope Paul VI was to write: 'It concerns the whole Church that the Order continues to flourish, for contemplation and prayer are to be valued as primary duties which profit the whole world.'

Further evidence of the immense treasure chest of love and prayer that is a Charterhouse can be found in some evocative comments made by the few visitors who have been able to spend a retreat, be it only for a day, within Carthusian walls. Here, selected at random, are some words of praise, and gratitude for beautiful experiences, which I garnered from the visitors' book at St Hugh's Charterhouse, Parkminster:

I would love to live and die here.

Precious peace and silence.

I have found here that peace which the world cannot give.

Thank God for such centres of prayer. He lives in a special way in the community.

Truly a place of healing. Thank you Fathers and Brothers for a lovely encounter with Christ.

This Heaven on Earth.

An unforgettable experience[1] [this phrase recurs over and over again].

---

[1] I recently met a senior Anglican priest who had spent twenty-four hours in a Charterhouse. He told me, quite unequivocally: 'It was the greatest experience of my life.'

[113]

Please God here I experienced the beginning of the exquisite taste of peace.

Thy will be done ... and here it is.

Now I know that I am loved, before I just hoped.

A milestone in my life. Much is said in silence.

Here I met the happiest people in the world.

An oasis in a crazy world.

The highlight of my life, such as may not recur.

My own favourite words were these written by a young man of eighteen who hoped to enter the Order as a Novice. Too young – no one under twenty can be accepted into the Novitiate – he had been sent away and told to re-apply in two years' time if he still felt he had a vocation. He wrote: 'Please God that in two years I may enter this house and never come out of it again.'

The Carthusian, like his 'ancestor' the Desert Father, does not seek to be 'extraordinary' by retiring from the world, but rather to be his ordinary self, true to God. This contrasts strongly with many men and women today, who drift along with the current accepted values, however debased, acquiring a lemming-like herd mentality, floundering on the road to disaster.

In our present age there is an almost desperate need for man to recapture just some of that 'experience' of simplicity and absolute truth which the early Christians found in the desert, the living tradition of which the Carthusians are the incarnate heirs. Peace is born of silence, because silence is the threshold where the soul meets God.

# PART THREE

# XVII

## CONTEMPLATION FOR ALL

Were the happiness of the next world as closely apprehended as the felicities of this, it were a martyrdom to live.

*Sir Thomas Browne, 1605–82*

I hope that no one who has followed the journey with me from the days of Abraham, St John the Baptist, the Desert Fathers and through nearly one thousand years of the Carthusian inheritance can fail to have been impressed by the transcendent spirituality of those mystic souls *par excellence* who dwell in Charterhouses. Were all mankind, by some divine miracle, able to detach itself from the world in the Carthusian way, it would surely be paradise regained. Short of such a miracle, the world could do with as many Charterhouses as possible pouring out prayer. All mankind cannot follow the Carthusian way of life, but it is not too lofty an aim for more of us to try to bring into our lives something of the spirit of Carthusian contemplation and detachment from earthly things.

Not only have saints, Desert Fathers and Carthusians pursued the path of contemplation while reaching for a higher state, but history shows that it has been a road followed by Jewish, Hindu and Buddhist mystics and one advocated by ancient Greek philosophers.

In the words of Aldous Huxley in *The Perennial Philosophy*: 'It is axiomatic that the end of human life is contemplation or the direct and intuitive awareness of God.' In this he was following the precept of the seventeenth-century German philosopher Leibnitz, who coined the phrase *'philosophia perennis'*, by which he meant that the truth of divine reality had been recognised ever since primitive times.

The Zen Buddhist's conception of Nirvana is a detachment from earthbound time into a state where time and eternity are one and the same. Hinduism, grown out of ancient Brahminism, with its pantheistic all-god Brahma, yet has something to offer all contemplatives – including Christian monks. So does Taoism, which aims at freedom from earthly passion and whose main proponent, Lao Tzu, said: 'Christians have no monopoly of mysticism.' As William James wrote: 'There is about mystical utterances an eternal unanimity which ought to make a critic stop and think.' But it is the certainty that God is a personal god, of self-giving love, to whom we become united by love, which radically differentiates Christian mysticism from that of the East.

The Greek thinkers, both Stoic and Platonistic, saw progress of moral life as a movement towards purity of mind, eventually so pure as to apprehend God. This vision, *'theoria'*, is equivalent to contemplation, but focuses on its intellectual aspect without giving sufficient attention to sharing the life of God through love.

In his book *Major Trends in Jewish Mysticism*, Gershom Scholem refers to the earliest Jewish mystics who spoke of 'the ascent of the soul to the celestial throne, where it obtains an ecstatic view of the majesty of God and the secrets of his realm.' Jewish mysticism gives birth to the conception of a sphere, a realm of divinity underlying the world of our sense, yet present and active in all that exists. This is what the Kabalists term the world of the *Sephirof*.[1] The Jewish mystic tries to assure himself of the living

---

[1] Kabalism is a system of occult theosophy or mystical interpretation of the Scriptures among Jewish rabbis. In Kabalistic writings, *Sephirof* refers to emanations and manifestations of the Godhead.

presence of God while not renouncing the idea of the hidden God, eternally unknowable in the depth of the mystic's own self, or, to use a Kabalistic expression – 'in the depths of his nothingness'.

Intuitive awareness of the divine reality can come to an individual in many ways: looking at a Leonardo or an El Greco painting, listening to a Beethoven sonata, reading a poem of William Blake, surveying the world from a mountain top, looking at the stars on a dark night, watching giant waves crashing against the rocks in a storm, tragedy in the shape of the death of a loved one. The hand of God is ever present, and often at such times, without realising it, the individual finds himself contemplating divine reality. But the sense of 'awareness' – or moment of truth as I have called it – can quickly vanish because in most cases that awareness, although intuitive from the heart, is unaccompanied by an effort of will and purpose.

To have an awareness of God in the heart is only of lasting value if accompanied by an awareness in the mind; 'mind' requires 'will' and 'will' requires 'discipline'. Through their discipline the Desert Fathers and the Carthusians did and do cast off all distractions of this world to bring both heart and will to contemplate the divine reality in its totality.

Man today is constantly seeking peace or solace of some kind in a hundred different ways – drugs, alcohol, cigarettes, television, sex, greed are all unceasingly encouraged by remorseless advertising which, to quote Aldous Huxley once more, 'has but one purpose – to prevent the will from ever achieving silence'. All vices can be summed up in the one vice of greed. Conquer greed and you conquer all other vices. Yet the prime aim of advertising is to pander to greed!

It is the power of advertising, too, which has brought many – particularly younger people dissatisfied with the purposelessness of twentieth-century western civilisation –

to seek quietude in meditative religious and quasi-religious cults or techniques, mostly stemming from the Orient. The best known of these in the West is transcendental meditation, which has made a great deal of money for some of its teachers.

Carthusians do not sell techniques; their life is devoted to God and not to smiling down on us from underground posters calling us to meetings in public halls where, in return for a suitably large cheque, we can receive a 'course' on meditation. Orthodox monks do not go to concert halls to instruct people on how to say the Jesus Prayer; they are far too occupied saying it themselves in solitude – alone with God.

The highest and most rewarding form of detachment is one in which one not only detaches one's heart and mind from this world, but also attaches them to something higher – divine reality. Human knowledge, says St Thomas Aquinas, begins with a sense of awareness. It does not come from merely syphoning off tension – helpful as this may be at times in its limited sphere – by cocooning oneself temporarily in a vacuum as the protagonists of transcendental meditation would have us do.

If one can spend just a little time each day in an endeavour to achieve some of that peace which the world cannot give, by making a contemplative approach to God as practised so effectively through the centuries, the benefit to the soul and one's mental and physical wellbeing could be immeasurable. It should not be too difficult to withdraw from time to time from ordinary occupations during the day and lift up one's heart to God, in the words of the Psalmist, and create that interior solitude which makes room for the voices of the divine. Peace and silence in the soul are synonymous: peace is born of silence because silence is the threshold where the soul meets God.

Ideally, every day – preferably at a fixed time soon after you awake – spend half an hour, say, in complete quiet and solitude; try to relax your whole body and put aside all distracting thoughts and cares of this world in preparation for contemplation. You may find it helpful, before you attempt to reach a contemplative state, to recite to yourself a simple affective prayer, such as: 'My God, I am as nothing. Let your love of me enter my soul and stay there.' Then, perhaps, spend a few minutes reflecting on the perfection of the lives of the Desert Fathers and of today's Carthusians, whose prayers of intercession for the world have been rising to heaven while you slept. Recall that both Moses and Christ laid down quite unequivocally that the first and greatest commandment was to love God with all your might, your whole heart, your whole mind and your whole soul.

Then choose a phrase, whichever appeals to you most, from the list of meditative thoughts set out in the next chapter, and ruminate on it. Mull it over in your heart and in your mind; let it flow into you, then out of you, then back into you again.

I once heard the artist Victor Passmore telling a class of students to get to the very essence and heart of things and paint what they felt. 'Imagine', he said, 'that you are the centre of a fir-cone; imagine that you are in the middle of a ball of string.' Adapt a similar attitude to the meditative thought you have chosen; try to think yourself right into it so that it becomes part of you and you part of it. Yet always beware of meditation on yourself, which can lead to introspection and its accompanying dangers.

Although an act of will is clearly involved in such contemplation, the heart also should be much immersed and, in time, it is the heart that will carry the soul forward to regions unknown to the intellect. In *The Ladder of Paradise*, St John Climacus gives excellent advice on disciplining the mind for contemplation:

If by constant practice you train your mind never to stray, it will be under your control even at meal times, but if it wanders at random and is not restrained you will never know where to find it. Listen to the words of the great hero of high and perfect prayer: 'I would rather speak with understanding, were it only five words' [St Paul's First Epistle to the Corinthians, 14:19]. Detach yourself from love for the world and its pleasures. Cast aside all care. Abandon your thoughts. Forget the body, for prayer is nothing else but this: to make oneself a stranger to the world, both visible and invisible.

Try to ensure that during your period of contemplation you have no interruptions, for, as St John of the Cross wrote: 'He who interrupts the course of his spiritual exercises and prayer is like a man who allows a bird to escape, he can hardly catch it again.'

Any serious and persistent effort to achieve a contemplative state will gradually yet certainly bear fruit, even though it may take some time to attain complete 'wordless prayer' or 'pure prayer'. Yet, as the weeks and months go by, you will find your mind more and more fixed on the mysteries of God. However, do remember that you will not necessarily make progress every single day towards a higher level of contemplation. It is not at all uncommon for God to raise souls up to a pinnacle and then to cast them down as part of the process of mortification. It happened to Christ himself.

In any event, never be in a hurry with God. 'Nothing is more important than to know how to wait on God,' wrote the Carthusian Dom Augustin Guillerand. 'Go slowly, or better still, keep in step with God who is never in a hurry.' When we first become aware of deep interior changes within ourselves we must learn to treasure the great peace of this personal possession of the truth.

You may wish to hold to the same meditative thought every day or to use a different one each day or change to a new one each week. There can be no fixed prescription in these matters: let your heart and inclination guide you.

[122]

Try to back up your fixed time for contemplation with little periods of prayer during the day. As Theophan[1] points out:

> The Jesus Prayer can be recited at any time in any place; bus queues, in the garden, the kitchen, dressing or walking, suffering from insomnia, moments of distress or mental strain. It is a prayer particularly well adapted to the tensions of the modern world. It is a prayer which fits every stage of the spiritual life from the most elementary to the most advanced.

St Francis de Sales' recommendation is: 'Keep your soul sitting down and at rest before God. While we are busily occupied with external affairs we must apply ourselves to the study of the tranquillity of the heart.'

One of the most simple of prayers – divine in its simplicity – is to make an act of faith, hope and love by just saying: 'Abba, Father'. Salutary and elevated, there is no prayer more certain than this.

It was the seventeenth-century Dominican Father Alexander Piny who wrote: 'We cannot always be united with God through thought because of distractions and tiredness etc., but we can always be united by love and by an act of will even when we are not thinking about God.'

Sometimes, to a rare few, contemplation can lead to what is called 'infused prayer' or the 'prayer of union', which is preceded by a period of a sense of complete inability to pray. St John of the Cross, describing this state, wrote: 'It means God wants them to stop praying so he can pray within their souls himself.'

St Teresa of Avila tells of how one of her lay sisters came to her one day to complain that she could not pray any more. St Teresa asked her why not, and the lay sister replied: 'I keep saying the "Our Father" over and over

---

[1] Theophan the Recluse (1815–94) was a Russian Orthodox monk who translated the Philokalia from the Greek into Russian.

[123]

again.' St Teresa realised that the lay sister had achieved the 'prayer of union', and was passing through the phase which St John of the Cross calls the 'night of the senses' or the 'night of the spirit' – a state which the soul reaches before the Holy Spirit takes over completely, a state which St Teresa herself experienced and described as 'the soul hurtling through space abandoned by God'. For those who pursue the path of sanctity to its ultimate, the soul attains a mysterious consummation beyond definition.

St Thomas Aquinas defined mysticism as '*Cognitio Dei experimentalis*', which is the knowledge of God through experience (compare Psalm 34, 'Oh, taste and see that the Lord is good.') Yet the world of the mystic cannot be expressed rationally except through paradox. And the paradox of the perception of truth is that in writing of the infinite it is impossible to produce in the man-made words of a finite world a wholly adequate simile or allegorical account.

The twentieth-century Father C. C. Martindale, SJ, wrote: 'Mystics are not only the ultimate source of our knowledge of the soul but are the salt which preserves human society from decay. God does not deprive the world of them for they are its sustainers. Dying to themselves, they become capable of perpetual inspiration, through a specially divine grace, to the pastoral ministry in the outside world.'

Modern, and not so modern, religious literature abounds with numerous definitions of categories and methods of prayer: 'active', 'passive', 'mental', 'meditative', 'formalised', 'vocal', 'silent', etc. Until the secular priesthood and the newer 'active' religious orders appeared on the scene, such as the Dominicans, Franciscans and Jesuits and greatly expanded formalised prayer, no definition of prayer was really required: prayer was synonymous with contemplation. Because of their active life, members of the new religious orders devised methods of prayer which aimed to cram into an hour or two prayers over which the Desert Fathers and the Carthusians would spend all day. In so doing, they have to some extent bedevilled the simple prayers devolved from the early Christians, thereby causing some confusion both to themselves and to others.

St Benedict never prescribed 'methods' of prayer, nor does he even mention the word 'meditation'. Prayer was prayer, and that was that. It is important to recall that the Eucharist of the early Christians in the desert was a simple affair in part resembling the Jewish Passover table blessing. The few prayers said in common were but a brief interruption to their life of contemplation or 'pure prayer'. Simplicity is the keyword. It is the lesson Christ taught us when he declared that the Kingdom of Heaven is for children and those that are childlike. When you devote yourself to contemplating divine reality, approach God in this spirit.

Cardinal Hume wrote: 'The only Orders never to have been affected by change are the established contemplatives. The basic elements of contemplative life are as relevant today as they have ever been.' God and the contemplatives, whom, as I pointed out earlier, Cardinal Hume refers to as 'the six per cent return on capital God has reserved for himself', seem to cry out to us for infinitely more prayer. Going to church on Sundays and doing good works are simply not enough. Not everyone is called to scale the Carthusian heights, but undoubtedly some who are called do not respond. Those who feel unable wholly to attain to the Carthusian ideal should not forget that there are other religious orders, and in some of the Benedictine congregations contemplation plays an important role.

Much of the life of 'active' priests today is devoted to many unrewarding tasks. With little time to live with God, to pray to and with him – the 'active' priest 'flies the flag'

[125]

for God in a largely hostile world. He needs more of the solid prayer offered up by such as the Carthusians to help him. Of conversions to Christianity the Jesuit Father Joseph Rickaby wrote: 'We should have more conversions if we did more penance to procure them. We must have some of our numbers to go apart and fast and pray and do penance for the rest of us. How can we fast and pray whose daily work suffers from lack of time and strength to do it?' All of us can help both our own progress to heaven and the works of priests in the world if we spend just part of our day in divine contemplation.

It would be quite wrong to suggest that Carthusians should come out into the world to teach us all how to try to live in contemplation of God. Were they to do so, it would be a descent from the heights to exchange the pure gold of silence for the base metal of words. This would destroy the whole foundation of their exemplary lives alone with God, which are such an inspiration to the rest of us. Perhaps, however, some cardinals, bishops and priests generally should find time to make regular retreats in Charterhouses – and the Carthusians open their doors a little wider to them – so that, having drunk at the well of the Carthusian spirituality, they can tell the world more about the joys of contemplation. However, I recognise that some Carthusians may not agree with this suggestion, and see it as a potential diminution of the effectiveness of their apostolate of solitary prayer.

Of all the active souls of this century Mother Teresa is perhaps the most beautiful. Few can have devoted themselves so totally to good works in the fullest meaning of the phrase. Yet for every group of her nuns and helpers there is a 'twin' house of contemplatives who do nothing but pray. Mother Teresa knows better than anyone that without this constant stream of unseen, unheard prayer her work would not be possible.

'I leave you peace ... my peace I give you.'

# XVIII

# WISDOM BEYOND UNDERSTANDING

Their words to the end of the world.

*Psalm 19, verse 4*

Here is a selection of timeless thoughts from various sources, but including many of Carthusian origin, on which to meditate. All can be aids toward reaching some degree of contemplation, but to each his own. Take one phrase or sentence a day or hold to the same one for a month, a year, or even a lifetime – no matter – just so long as it helps you toward God, the peace of truth and pure prayer for part of each day and – hopefully, as time goes on – a greater part of each day.

*Ecce eris Tacens!* (Behold thou shall be silent.)
Luke 1: 20

Give me a mind serene for contemplation.
John Gay, 1685–1732

Perfection consists of holding fast to very great simplicity.
Abbé de Tourville, 1842–1903,
*Letters of Direction*

Where are we to find happiness? In God alone. He hides himself in all created things from which we ask happiness and which cannot give it to us. They are the veil which hides the infinite beauty of his face. When we pass beyond

[127]

the veil to meet reality which is behind it all, there are we consoled and our joy is full.

Dom Augustin Guillerand, O. Cart., 1877–1945

Beyond finite beauty – that is the beauty that we see – is a depth of infinite beauty from which all created beauty comes.

Augustin Guillerand

O holy solitude, happy beyond measure, who may tell your praises! O life, sweetness, rest, shelter, path of retreat.

Paul Giustiniani, 1476–1528, founder of the Camaldolese hermits of Monte Carona

Happy the soul that obtains that peace that never comes except by loving only God and only for his own sake.

Paul Giustiniani

The prayer of the heart introduces us into deep interior silence so that we learn to experience its power. For that reason the prayer of the heart has always to be very simple, confined to the simplest of acts and often making use of no words and no thoughts at all.

Thomas Merton

Oh taste and see that the Lord is good.

Psalm 34, verse 9

He who is granted the supreme experience, loses the reality of his intellect. But when he returns from such contemplation he finds it full of divine inflowing splendour.

Rabbi Levi Isaac of Berditchev

We need silence to be able to touch souls. The essential thing is not what we say but what God says to us and through us.

Father Karl Rahner, SJ

Men who have no other purpose in life but God. Is there any other purpose for anyone?

The Rule of St Benedict

True simplicity is to attach yourself to God alone, for in him you will find everything. The saints were, and are, eminently simple.

Abbé de Tourville

Wisdom's self oft seeks to sweet retired solitude where with her best nurse contemplation. . . .

John Milton, *Comus*

All meditation, knowledge and consideration of created things should bring us to contemplate the Divine on which all our attention should be fixed.

Denis the Carthusian

Truth must be the last end of the whole universe and the consideration thereof must be the chief occupation of wisdom.

St Thomas Aquinas, *c*. 1225–74

The First Philosophy is the knowledge of truth, not any truth but truth which is the source of all truth.

St Thomas Aquinas

God is a sheer absolute one, sundered from all two-ness, and in whom we must eternally sink from nothingness to nothingness.

Johannes Eckhart, *c*. 1260–1327

Those who do not perceive God purely and simply as the ONE, injure not God, of course, but themselves and, along with themselves, their fellows.

Philo of Alexandria, *c*. 13 BC–AD 50

Not in the midst of life's tumult nor in the world of pleasure's round does God show himself, but in the inspiration of nature, grace, light as a breath of fresh air in a still small voice.

St Jerome

They are on the way to Truth who apprehend God by means of divine light.

St John of the Cross

From good men goodness may be learned.

Aristotle, 384–322 BC

The truth is that God alone is wise, and wise omniscience is letting us know that the wisdom of most men is worth little or nothing.

Socrates, 470–399 BC

The contemplative life in itself, by its very nature is superior to the active life.

St Thomas Aquinas

A very little of this pure love is more precious to the sight of God and of more profit to the Church, even though the soul appears to be doing nothing, than are all other works put together.

St John of the Cross

The right relationship between prayer and conduct, is not that conduct is supremely important and prayer may help it, but that prayer is supremely important and conduct tests it.

William Temple, Archbishop of Canterbury, 1881–1944

He who knows does not speak
He who speaks does not know.

Lao Tzu, *c.* 600 BC

How foolish and how blind you are, intoxicated by worldly pleasure and honour. You forget the delights of Heaven and the glories of the celestial realm.

Paul Giustiniani

[130]

Men immersed in worldly affairs should not say that solitaries are inactive or idle. If by idle they mean that hermits neither buy nor sell, nor build, nor navigate, nor engage in law suits, nor raise children, then such a condemnation would likewise apply to the holy angels of God.

Paul Giustiniani


Let me know myself. Let me know thee.

St Augustine, died *c.* 605


Be still and know that I am God.

Psalm 46, verse 10


It is because it is simple that a soul is still.

Augustin Guillerand


No-one in this life is proof against temptations and faults, but when by an excess of divine goodness our gaze penetrates the mystery of the divine filiation in us, we cannot feel fear. Such a soul laughs at life and death and at the idea of the present and the future, at principalities and powers, for its joy is vaster than all the oceans and its peace deeper than all the depths.

Augustin Guillerand


It happens to some souls to whom God may have chosen to extend his grace, that they have a greater experience of the indwelling of God and that sacramental communion is less important. The mystery of grace given through mystical experience can never be explained. We only know it happens to certain souls who may be in all sorts of walks of life.

Abbé de Tourville


God is in space without space and in time without time.

Emmanuel Swedenborg, 1689–1772


When infinite Wisdom teaches, the truth is grasped in a

[131]

moment and there is no delay in learning nor need of reasoning.

> Dom Michael of Coutances, Minister-General of the
> Carthusian Order, died 1600

So beware of behaving in a manner seeking wild enjoyment, but learn to love God with the quiet joy that rests in body and soul.

> *The Cloud of Unknowing*[1]

Perfection consists in holding fast to the very greatest simplicity. Simplicity is the final word as regards the true way of living. It is the lesson Our Lord teaches us when he declares that the Kingdom of Heaven was for children and those that are childlike.

> Abbé de Tourville

Of course it is better to say 'Our Father', with all the depth of understanding of the words, than to repeat the Lord's Prayer twelve times.

> Archbishop Anthony Bloom, Metropolitan of Surozh and
> Exarch of the Russian Patriarch in Western Europe

There are times when we do not need any words of prayer, neither our own nor anyone else's, and then we pray in perfect silence. This perfect silence is the ideal prayer.

> Augustin Guillerand

If only men could see more deeply, they would find what a treasure is hidden in solitude and everyone would run to it.

> Dom Johannes Lanspergus, Carthusian, 1490–1539

When then does the soul light on the truth? When nothing

---

[1] *The Cloud of Unknowing*, by an anonymous author, is probably the most spiritual book to be written in the English language. It was written in the fourteenth century and is believed to be either by a Carthusian monk or by a hermit priest in contact with the Carthusians. A sixteenth-century manuscript in the hand of the Carthusian martyr William Exmew is at St Hugh's Charterhouse, Parkminster.

disturbs it. Neither hearing, nor sight nor pain, nor pleasure of any kind. And when it retires as much as possible within itself, taking leave of the body, and as far as it can, not communicating, or being in contact with it, it aims at the discovery of that which is the truth.

Plato

Contemplation is that raising up whereby the mind is wrapt in God and tastes of the sweetness of eternal joy.

Guiges II, 9th Prior of La Grande Chartreuse, *c.* 1115–90

Many difficulties are really created by ourselves, we hurry and worry, and almost think it a virtue to be impatient. The best way to overcome a difficulty is certainly not to worry. The saints did not become perfect in a day, it took them a long time to overcome all their difficulties. But they were amazingly cheerful.

Father Daniel Considine, SJ

The discovery of Wisdom is the surpassing good. When this is found, all the people will sing.

Philo of Alexandria

Commune with your heart and be still.

Psalm 4, verse 4

Prayer is essentially simple and is tantamount to standing before God with the mind in the heart.

Theophan the Recluse, *c.* 1815–94

To many people the saints seem far from us. But the saints are far only from those who have taken themselves away from them.

Staretz Silovan, monk of Mount Athos, 1866–1938

Therefore leave your soul, too, to pray as it suits it best in its own way. Most important however is to allow it to remain still.

Augustin Guillerand

We pray in secret when from the heart and fervent mind we disclose our petitions to God alone. Wherefore we should pray in complete silence not only to avoid distracting the brethren standing near by our whispers or utterances and disturbing the thoughts of those who are praying, but also that the purport of our petition may be concealed.

Cassian

We should enter into conversation with God without troubling about the composition of our words.
Dom Le Masson, Minister-General of the Carthusian Order, 1628–1703

Those souls which are completely occupied by God have nothing to say since their interior being is everything and contains everything they could wish to say.
Dom Le Masson

Contemplation is the act of the soul wrapped in admiration in the presence of something more beautiful than itself.
Augustin Guillerand

Prayer is nothing else in my opinion but being on terms of friendship with God.
St Teresa of Avila

The naked soul will adhere to naked Truth, having no need for any speech, any analogy or any example to grasp it.

Guiges

The soul advances not so much by thinking but by loving much.
St Teresa of Avila

The contemplative soul is an enclosed garden where one has the joy of receiving directly the divine life in the stillness comparable to that which doubtless reigned at the dawn of the world.

Augustin Guillerand

The contemplative life directly and immediately occupies itself with the love of God in which there is no act more perfect or more meritorious. Indeed that love is the root of all merit. The contemplative life stablishes a man in the very heart of all spiritual fecundity.

St Thomas Aquinas

O thou who art at home
Deep in my heart
Enable me to join you
Deep in my heart.

The Talmud

The Father only spoke but once; it was his Word. He spoke it eternally and in eternal silence. It is in silence that the soul will hear it.

St John of the Cross

Only experience reveals what benefits the solitude and silence of the desert bring to those who love it.

St Bruno

# POPE JOHN PAUL II'S MESSAGE TO THE CARTHUSIANS ON THEIR 900th ANNIVERSARY

*To Our Dear Son Andrew Poisson, Minister-General of the Carthusian Order*

'To be devoted to the silence and the solitude of the Cell' is recognised as the principal endeavour and goal of the Carthusian Order, of which you are the Head. Its members, responding to a special call from God and in order to live for Him alone, have passed 'from the tempest of this world to the safety and peace of a sheltered post' (S. Bruno, 'Letter to Raoul', *Sources chrétiennes*).

For now nine hundred years your Order has endeavoured with praiseworthy energy and perseverance to lead this 'life hidden with Christ'. This is fittingly recalled at the present time when the memory of its origin is being celebrated. For the Order was founded about June 24 in the year 1084 – a day consecrated to St John Baptist, 'the greatest of the prophets and lover of the desert' – he, whom the Carthusians honour, after the Blessed Virgin Mary, as their heavenly Patron. It was then that a most eminent man, St Bruno, and a few companions, commenced that form of life, separated from the world, in a place called La Chartreuse, in the diocese of Grenoble.

We rejoice together with you from the bottom of our heart in commemorating this happy occasion. We heartily congratulate you for so long a fidelity and wish to mark it by expressing our special esteem and paternal affection to the entire Carthusian family.

As is well known, in the early ages of the Church hermits were to be found dedicated to prayer and work in the desert. 'Stripped of all, they gave name to a heavenly form of life' (St Athanasius, *Life of St Antony*). It was they who founded the

[137]

religious life itself. Their example provoked admiration, and drew many men to the path of virtue. St Jerome, to cite but one of many witnesses, proclaimed, with inflamed passion, the hidden lives of these monks: 'O desert, shining with the flowers of Christ! O solitude, in which are born those stones with which in the Apocalypse is built the city of the great king! O desert place, rejoicing with greater familiarity with God!' (*Letter 14*)

The Roman Pontiffs have approved this life of separation many times, and commended it with praise. As regards yourselves, in contemporary times there has been the Apostolic Constitution 'Umbratilem' of Pius XI, and the Letter of Paul VI sent to you on the occasion of your General Chapter. For its part, the Vatican Council II has extolled the solitary life, whose adherents follow more closely Christ in contemplation on the mountain and has declared it to be the hidden source of fecundity of the Church. Finally, the new Code of Canon Law clearly confirms this teaching: 'Institutes which are wholly directed to contemplation have always had a choice position in the mystical Body of Christ.'

All this concerns you, dear Carthusian monks and nuns who, far from the tumult of the world, 'have chosen the better part' (cf. Luke 10:41). Confronted by the increased pace of life which presses on our contemporaries, you must return continually to the original spirit of your Order and remain unshaken in your holy way of life. Our epoch seems to need the example you set in your life of devotion. People today are bombarded by various conflicting streams of thought and are frequently troubled by these. They are exposed to spiritual dangers by so much of what is published indiscriminately – especially by the media, which have such great power to influence men's hearts, often contrary to Christian truth and morality. Mankind needs to seek the absolute, and to see it confirmed, as it were, by a living witness. It is your task to show them this. For their part, those sons and daughters of the Church who devote themselves to the apostolate in the world, in the midst of changing and transient things, need to rest in the stability of God and His love. This stability they see manifested in you who, during this earthly pilgrimage, possess it in an especial way. The Church, as the mystical Body of Christ, owes it to herself to offer continually to the divine Majesty a sacrifice of praise and it is one of her chief duties. She relies on your zealous devotion – on you who are daily 'occupied in the divine services' (cf. St Bruno, *Letters*). However, it must be acknowledged that in these days, when perhaps too much importance is given to activity, the value of your eremitic life is sometimes insufficiently understood, or underestimated – particularly when so many workers are needed in the Lord's vineyard. Against such views it has to be asserted that the Carthusians must fully preserve the authentic character of their Order, even in our own days. This accords with the norm of the new Code of Canon Law which, while recalling the urgent need of the active apostolate, defends the special vocation of those who are members of entirely contemplative religious institutions – precisely because of the service they render to the people of God 'whom they move by their example, and contributing to their increase through a hidden apostolic fruitfulness'. If, for this reason, your members 'cannot be called upon to assist in the various pastoral ministries', neither should you, at least not habitually, exercise that other form of apostolate, which consists in giving hospitality to people from the outside world who wish to make a few days' retreat, since that is not in accord with your eremitic vocation.

Without doubt the many and rapid changes which take place in modern society produce deep psychological effects – particularly among the young – and are the cause of that nervous tension from which so many people suffer today. They may also cause difficulties in Carthusian communities, principally among those who aspire to join your Order. For this reason, it is necessary to act prudently and firmly – while taking into account the problems facing the young – so that your true charism may remain intact, without any departure from your approved Statutes. Only a will enflamed with the love of God and prepared to serve him zealously in the austerity of a life removed from the company of men, can overcome these obstacles.

The Church is close to you, dear sons and daughters of Saint Bruno; she depends on the great spiritual fruits resulting from your prayers and austerities you bear for love of God. We have already said elsewhere, explaining the life consecrated to God:

[139]

'It is not so important what you do, but what you are'. This seems to apply in a special way to you, who are withdrawn from what is called the active life.

While you recall in your hearts the origins of your family, you cannot help but be moved to a renewal of that interior ardour and spiritual joy which you give without restraint to your sublime vocation.

As a sign of the love which has inspired us to write these lines, and as a token of abundant celestial graces, we rejoice in the Lord to grant the Apostolic Blessing to you, dear Son, and to all the Monks and Nuns of the Carthusian Order.

From the Vatican, 24 May 1984, the sixth year of our Pontificate.

(sig.) John Paul II

On the eve of St Bruno's feast day, 6 October 1984, Pope John Paul II made a pilgrimage to La Torre to visit the Carthusians and to pray at St Bruno's tomb. In an address to the monks extolling the Carthusian life the Pope said:

> From your faces one can see how God gives the peace and joy of the Spirit as a reward to whoever has left everything to live by him and sing his praises for ever. . . . My hope is that from this place a message may go out to the world and reach especially the young people, opening before their eyes the perspective of the contemplative life as a gift from God.

# TIMETABLE OF A DAY IN THE LIFE OF A CARTHUSIAN FATHER

Although there may be slight variations in times in different countries, the following sets out a typical day for a father in a charterhouse.

| | |
|---|---|
| 11.45 p.m. | Rise. |
| 12.00 midnight | Little Office of Our Lady. |
| 12.15 a.m. | Matin/Lauds (in church). |
| 2.45 a.m. | Little Office of Our Lady. Sleep (in cell). |
| 6.45 a.m. | Rise. |
| 7.00 a.m. | Little Office of Our Lady. Prime (in cell). |
| 7.30 a.m. | Spiritual exercises (in cell). |
| 8.00 a.m. | Little Office of Our Lady. Terce (in cell). |
| 8.15 a.m. | Conventual Mass (in church).[1] |
| 10.00 a.m. | Spiritual exercises (in cell). |
| 11.15 a.m. | Little Office of Our Lady. Sexte (in cell). |
| 11.30 a.m. | Dinner (in cell). |
| 12.30 p.m. | Relaxation. Cleaning of cell, mending etc. (in cell). |
| 1.15 p.m. | Little Office of Our Lady. Nones (in cell). |
| 1.30 p.m. | Spiritual exercises (in cell); also, perhaps, some gardening, cutting firewood etc. |
| 3.30 p.m. | Little Office of Our Lady (in cell). |

[1] Individual Masses in private are also said by the Fathers at times of their own choosing.

| | |
|---|---|
| 3.45 p.m. | Vespers (in church). |
| 4.15 p.m. | Spiritual exercises (in cell). |
| 6.45 p.m. | Angelus (in cell). |
| 7.15 p.m. (approx.) | Compline (in cell). |
| 8.00 p.m. | Sleep (in cell). |

Spiritual exercise is an all-embracing expression of the interior life equivalent to private contemplation, and covers all forms of prayer, *lectio divina*, religious study etc. In practice, the Carthusian life of contemplative prayer approximates to that of the Desert Fathers. Monastic meditation, prayer and contemplation, study and *lectio divina* all involve the whole man. Proceeding from his heart, they embrace his entire being at every level.

On Sundays and on weekdays on the occasion of solemn feast days, such as Christmas, Easter Monday and All Saints' Day, there is concelebrated Mass in the church at 8.45 a.m. instead of 8.15 a.m., and the offices of Terce and Sexte also take place in church. On these days Fathers and Brothers have their midday meal in the refectory – in strict silence except for the reading of a passage from the Scriptures or from the writings of the Fathers of the Church. On these days, also, all the monks assemble in the chapter house during the afternoon before Vespers for a reading from the Scriptures, from the Statutes or, perhaps once a month, for a sermon by the Prior or by someone delegated by him.

# THE CHARTERHOUSES IN 1984

## For Monks

**FRANCE**

La Grande Chartreuse, St Laurent du Pont, Isère.

Chartreuse de Notre-Dame de Montrieux, Meounes les Montrieux, La Roquebrussanne, Var.

Chartreuse de Notre-Dame de Portes, Benonces, Serrières de Briord, Ain.

Chartreuse de Selignac, Simandre-sur-Suran, Ain.

**GERMANY**

Karthaus Marienau, Bad Würzach, Württemberg.

**ITALY**

Certosa San Stefano et San Bruno, Serra San Bruno, Calabria.

Certosa di Farneta, Maggiano, Lucca.

**PORTUGAL**

Cartuxa Scala Coeli, Evora-Codex.

**SPAIN**

Cartuja de Aula Dei, Zaragoza.

Cartuja de la Defension, Jerez de la Frontera, Cadiz.

Cartuja de Miraflores, Burgos.

Cartuja de Montalegre, Tiana, Barcelona.

Cartuja de Porta Coeli, Serra, Valencia.

**SWITZERLAND**

Chartreuse de la Valsainte, La Valsainte, Fribourg.

**UNITED KINGDOM**

St Hugh's Charterhouse, Partridge Green, Horsham, Sussex.

**UNITED STATES**

Charterhouse of the Transfiguration, Arlington, Vermont.

YUGOSLAVIA
Kartuzija Pleterje, Sentjernej, Slovenia.

## For Nuns

FRANCE
Chartreuse Notre-Dame, Reillanne, Alpes de
    Haute-Provence.
Chartreuse du Précieux Sang, Nonenque, Marnhagues et
    Latour, Aveyron.

ITALY
Certosa di Riva, Via Vecchia di Piscina, Riva di Penerola,
    Turin.
Certosa di San Francesco, Giaveno, Turin.
Certosa di Vedana, Sospirolo (BL).

SPAIN
Cartuja de Benifaça, Castellon de la Plana, Tarragona.

# APPENDIX 4

## BIBLIOGRAPHY AND FURTHER READING

Several important source references have not been listed, as they are only to be found in a Charterhouse.

*The Call of the Desert*, Peter Anson: SPCK, 1964

*The Quest for Solitude*, Peter Anson: J. M. Dent, 1932

*The Life of St Antony*, St Athanasius (translated by R. T. Meyer): Newman Press, Maryland, USA, 1950

*The Cloud of Unknowing*, Anon: Penguin, 1976

*Holy Wisdom (Sancta Sophia)*, Augustine Baker, OSB: Burns and Oates, 1964

*Living Prayer*, Archbishop Anthony Bloom: Libra Books, 1966

*Three Mystics*, Bruno de J.M., ODC: Sheed and Ward, 1939

*The Spirituality of the New Testament and the Fathers*, Louis Bouyer: Burns and Oates, 1960

*The Contemplative Life*, A Carthusian: Burns and Oates, 1952

*The Prayer of Love and Silence*, A Carthusian: Darton Longman Todd, 1962

*Introduction à la Vie Intérieure*, A Carthusian of Valsainte: Audin et Cie, Lyon, 1941

*The Art of Prayer*, Igumen Chariton of Valamo: Faber and Faber, 1966

*The Passion and Martyrdom of the Holy English Carthusians*, Maurice Chauncey, O. Cart.: SPCK, 1935

*A Link between Flemish Martyrs and English Martyrs*, C. S. Durrant: Burns, Oates and Washbourne, 1925

*Where Silence is Praise*, Augustine Guillerand, O. Cart.: Darton Longman Todd, 1962

*They Speak by Silences*, Augustine Guillerand, O. Cart.: Darton, Longman Todd, 1978

*The Fathers of the Church* (Volume I), Francis X. Glimm,

Joseph M. F. Marique, SJ, Gerald C. Walsh, SJ: Catholic University of America Press, Washington, 1979

*Christian Perfection and Contemplation,* Father R. Garrigou-Lagrange, OP: B. Herder Book Co, St Louis, USA, 1946

*An Introduction to the Study of Ascetical and Mystical Theology,* Archbishop Alban Goodier, SJ: Burns, Oates and Washbourne, 1938

*The Perennial Philosophy,* Aldous Huxley: Chatto and Windus, 1946

*Writings from the Philokalia,* Trans. E. Kadloubovsky and G. E. H. Palmer: Faber and Faber, 1951

*Early Fathers from the Philokalia,* Trans. E. Kadloubovsky and G. E. H. Palmer: Faber and Faber, 1956

*The Monastic Orders in England,* David Knowles, OSB: Cambridge University Press, 1950

*Christian Monasticism,* David Knowles, OSB: Weidenfeld & Nicolson, 1969

*What is Mysticism?,* David Knowles, OSB: Burns and Oates, 1974

*Alone with God,* J. Leclercq, OSB: Catholic Book Club, 1961

*The Love of Knowledge and the Desire of God,* J. Leclercq, OSB: Fordham University Press, New York, 1961

*Carthusians,* J. D. Lee: Henry VI Society, 1981

*St Bruno et l'Ordre des Chartreux,* F. A. Lefevre: Librairie Catholique Internationale, 1883

*The London Charterhouse,* Dom Lawrence: Kegan Paul, 1889

*Upon God's Holy Hills,* C. C. Martindale, SJ: Washbourne, 1919

*Spiritual Reading for Every Day* (Volumes I and II), Dom Le Masson: Burns and Oates, 1962

*The Reformation and the Contemplative Life,* Archbishop David Mathew, Gervase Mathew, OP: Sheed and Ward, 1934

*Contemplative Meditation for All,* Father Matthew, ODC: Catholic Truth Society, 1979

*The Wisdom of the Desert,* Thomas Merton: Sheldon Press, 1979

*Tyburn, Hill of Glory,* The Nuns of Tyburn Convent: Burns and Oates, 1953

*Dizionario degli Instituti de Perfezione* (Volume II), Edited by

Guerrino Pellicia and Giancarlo Rocca: Edizione Paoline, Rome, 1975

*Major Trends in Jewish Mysticism*, Gershom G. Scholem: Thames & Hudson, 1955

*A Select Library of Nicene and Post Nicene Fathers* (Volume XI), Edited by Philip Schaff and Henry Ware: W. B. Ordmans Publishing Co, 1973

*Wisdom from Mount Athos*, Archimandrite Sophrony: Mowbrays, 1974

*The Carthusian Order in England*, Margaret Thompson: Macmillan, 1930

*Letters of Direction*, Abbé de Tourville: Amate Press, 1939

*The White Paradise*, Peter van de Meer: David McKay Inc, New York, 1952

*The Power of the Name: The Jesus Prayer and Orthodox Spirituality*, Archimandrite Kallistes Ware: S.L.G. Press, Oxford, 1974

# INDEX